Growing *The Whole Way*

D1243774

Using Your Whole Self to Create Lasting Change

Lauri Maynard, M.A., L.M.H.C.

Growing
The Whole Way

Growing
The Whole Way

A Three Phase Process:

Clarify what you want in your life

Learn how your past can help you move forward

Plan and Problem Solve more efficiently with all parts of yourself

Lauri Maynard

PUBLISHER'S INFORMATION

Author contact:

GrowingTheWholeWay.com

ISBN 978-1-7328387-0-3

Self-Help Techniques

© 2018 by Lauri Maynard

About the Artists:

Stephania Adler- Cover Art. From an early age, Stephania would use drawing as a way in which to express herself, when words were would fall short of what was in her heart. Many people have been deeply touched by her work, and always remark at how Stephania truly captured the essence of the subject. Requests for commissioned pieces are welcome via email at artworkbystephania@gmail.com.

Forrest Joss -Interior Tree Illustrations.

Brett Lehrman - Graphic Design. Brett is an American designer, artist, and musician whose works cover a wide range of mediums. His every work embodies the ethos of simplicity, efficiency, function, integrity, pleasant aesthetic, and providing joy. For more information and examples please visit BrettBrett.com.

A Note to Coaches and Counselors

This workbook is intended to be distributed to your clients as a way to teach, organize and support the work you are doing in a meaningful way. You and your client fill in the blanks to create a tangible resource to use both in and outside of treatment. The workbook is set up as an open structure which allows any client goal or therapeutic specialty to fit onto a plan that teaches:

- The overall process of change
- Whole Self awareness
- Meaningful action development
- Supportive self-care strategies
- Key concepts on how to think bigger and utilize the Mind, Body and Spirit to make changes last

For further study and information see:

Growing The Whole Way
A Teaching Guide for Coaches and Counselors

This workbook teaches about what holism is and how to foster that perspective in your work. It also instructs how to best utilize the Growing The Whole Way structure to ground client goals, organize the process needed for change, and assess what clients need after sessions are complete.

You will learn:

- How to align the program to your specialty and meet client specific needs.
- What is behind the key concepts that help your clients think bigger so that you can effectively teach them.
- Strategies on how to use holism to increase client motivation and follow through.
- Helpful tips to work with your own self-care and efficiency in your work.

For more information on using this program contact
Lauri Maynard at GrowingTheWholeWay.com

Books also available for purchase at Amazon.com

Acknowledgments

This book has been such a journey for me and could never have been conceived without the support and encouragement of so many invaluable people.

I am deeply grateful to my children, the most profound teachers I will ever know. Nicholas you showed me not only that unconditional love really does exist but also that I deserve nothing less. You literally turned my life around. Thank you for being such a powerful example. Rhianna you helped me to "be the animal." Your strength forced me to challenge myself, stand up for what I need and go after what I want. Thank you for pushing me forward.

I also cannot thank enough all those who worked with me on developing my ideas and putting them into practice. I appreciate your courage in facing that trial and error process. If not for your input this book would have never been completed. I especially want to personally acknowledge those that gave extra time to make this work a reality.

Cady, thanks for being the inspiration behind the 3D To Do List and for volunteering to write about your pivotal moments that later became the basis for the Learning Curves section. You were so patient with my tangents. Kyle I thank you for all your help in reshaping the workbook questions to be much more user friendly and efficient. You are naturally gifted in seeing the difference between what I really needed and what I just needed to say "f**k it" to. Marybeth I really appreciate all your help interpreting the process from a coaching perspective. It was very inspiring to see the depth of the system work when clinical needs weren't the central focus. Karen, special thanks to you for being the first brave soul to trial the system as a whole and graduate. Your input really helped to shape the landscape that tied each section together and encouraged me to keep moving with the concept.

I would also like to thank all those responsible for putting together this final product.

To Victoria for all her work in the early design drafts. It was the perfect starting place for my work to evolve.

To Marian, for her contributions to the General Mood Lifting Ideas as well as her gracious support in helping me build my own private practice. Many thanks for really being there over the years both as a professional and more importantly a friend.

To Brett, for all those late night creative sessions getting the worksheets and graphic work done. Thank you so much for your upbeat attitude and your patience with my many changes.

To Forrest, for your beautiful illustrations. I appreciate your added detail and personal flair.

To Mike for all your help with the edits. I appreciate your humor and attention to the details I couldn't see clearly.

To Rob for being the push I needed to get through that dreaded last 20% of the job. Thank you picking things up when they were rocky and not only getting me organized but also coming through as a true friend.

Finally, I cannot forget my deep gratitude for the friends and family who supported my own growth and learning.

Thanks to my parents who, in addition to life's essentials, provided the perfect environment for me to develop into the person I am today. I appreciate you both supporting me through school and being there for Nick and Rhianna. I couldn't have done it without you.

Many thanks to my friends who provided fun times and just the right support to keep me going. Thank you Kim and Amy for coordinating our monthly socials. The No Book/Book Club has taught me a lot!

Namaste to my spiritual supports who helped me find peace where I might otherwise miss it. Karyn and Randi I thank you so much for walking with me as I explore who I really am and what really matters. You both have been great friends, mentors and even therapists depending on the day.

Angela thank you so much for being such a great cheerleader. I appreciate you knowing just what I needed whether it was loving support or a good kick in the ass.

To Jim, the medium. I much appreciate your friendship, your soulful support and for connecting me to the book cover artist.

Thank you Peggy for dropping everything and showing up when I really need. Giving up your time, your apartment and just being there without me asking is much appreciated.

Thanks to Sarah, my adventurous friend, who is not afraid to try something new and encourages me to do the same. I appreciate you being the coach I need when I doubt myself and for many years keeping my hair in good style.

Much appreciation to Allison my cousin, my best friend and my life long support. I so appreciate your wisdom especially our favorite "Someday we are going to look back on this and laugh!" Thank you so much for never giving up on me and giving me the strength not to give up on myself.

Growing The Whole Way

TABLE OF CONTENTS

The Story Behind the Tree

The seed for this book idea came about ten years ago when I was struggling to organize myself around building my career. Back then I was facing divorce with two small children and realizing that I was not going to get much support. I was soon to be on my own and did not have the income to pay the bills I had in front of me. I had just finished my Master's degree in Holistic Counseling and was in a Certificate of Advanced Graduate Study program to earn credits toward state licensure as a Mental Health Counselor. I was also supervising a program for a mental health agency full time and doing additional clinical internship hours. Having worked in a variety of agency settings for many years, my goal was to have my own practice as a counselor. I knew I couldn't do clinical work because I was still gathering my credentials but I could through my Holistic Counseling degree do Spiritual Counseling and coach people toward meeting their goals. With my management experience, I also knew enough to assess a situation and make a referral if someone needed more intense services.

As I was putting together my ideas for my own practice I noticed a rental space ad above our local book store. I immediately felt charged about the idea of having a space and went to look at it. As soon as I walked in I knew I was meant to be there. The room had an old fireplace, a beautiful view of the town park and plenty of room to do both individual and group sessions. I don't know how, but I knew I was supposed to have my own space to do my own work. That day I drained my savings of the last $450 I had to put down for a deposit. I then sat down on the floor in my new empty room to meditate and felt compelled to write my mission. I wanted to focus my energy on what I was meant to do there. I wasn't clear of the details but I felt very strongly that this was a solid beginning to a solid career.

What I wrote that day was the poem at the end of this story. Usually poems take me sometime to write and evolve over many changes. This one did not. It took about twenty minutes and came in mostly one shot. Afterward, I changed only a few words to help the flow. Looking it over, I knew it felt right. Not understanding it fully I couldn't nail down a title so I ended up leaving it unnamed and framing it as it was.

With this mission I began to think in terms of what I was going to offer my clients. I thought about what people might need and came up with an idea of combining the Holistic Model I learned in school with goal setting and making things happen in life. At that time I was looking at it from a business standpoint. I invited two partners in and we set up a plan with a board of advisors. We hired a business consultant and I took a class on writing a business plan. My goal was to have a place for people to come and build on their potential. They would receive an assessment with an action plan and then we would help make referrals and have groups to support whatever they might need in their process. It was a big endeavor and I quickly realized too big for one person. I didn't have any start-up capital or steady income to support this non-profit organization. With my divorce around the corner I also did not have three to five years to allow it to grow. We then started looking at grants and from there things started to go badly. One of my partners had to leave because of family commitments and the other, along with myself, started to doubt our plan. In the end, I was left on my own and had to decide what to do. I fell back on my original gut feeling and forged ahead. Over the next few months things continued to lead nowhere. There was no money coming in and I was losing my momentum. The last straw was my computer hard drive crashing which took most of my notes with it. It had been a year, I had hit the end as far as I was concerned and I was devastated. How could something that felt so right go so very wrong?

The beauty of hindsight has since helped me answer that question and in doing so has laid the foundation for the workbook you have in front of you. Back then I understood the concept of holism but hadn't had enough life experience to really put it into practice. I didn't understand that I was not operating as a whole person when I was trying to develop my business. I knew what my gut was trying to tell me but it wasn't lining up with my feelings. I was operating out of fear. My feelings were about survival. Remember, I was trying to make a go of it as an income to provide for my children. My agenda was as much about helping myself as it was about helping others. When I was operating out of fear my logic seemed to make sense but didn't grasp the whole picture because it was limited by those fears. I couldn't know that at the time because my fear had narrowed my thinking. Now I can see that fear kept me focused on the money instead of on the purpose my gut was originally pointing to. I also didn't consider how my reality was supposed to hold up such an idea. How can I, as one person, really provide such a vast well rounded service? My timing was way off. I had a vision which my spirit accurately identified but I didn't have the resources yet to pull it off. My body was not capable of taking on such a project living the reality I was living at that time. My mind was too distracted by the stress of managing my family's basic needs so I couldn't be effective as a leader in the work. How could I walk with someone through their journey if I hadn't walked enough of my own?

Since then I've done a lot of personal growth work on myself. I have also completed the requirements and now have been practicing as a licensed Mental Health Counselor for 10 years. I still use the principles of my original idea and have now written them down in a system. Instead of going for the big business way of providing this service I am doing it one person at a time. Instead of providing a plan of action I am empowering people to write their own. I am helping people to see and grow into their own potential. My mind is now less fearful, which gives me space to think more about what I have to offer, instead of focusing on what I need to get by. My body is equipped with more experience and awareness which has helped me to understand and write down the system I am offering. My spirit, throughout, has remained fairly consistent. There were times when I doubted myself and gave up, but each time I started again my gut had the same message that always comes back to my mission in the poem. At this moment I have a better sense of where I have been and what I want now. I still have to work out the details of moving forward but I feel confident I have the wisdom to know what is best for me, and can access it when I look at my whole self, instead of just my fear.

My poem has traveled with me through two agencies and four office spaces before it has landed where I am now, in a successful full time practice. At this point I understand that I couldn't name the poem back then because it wasn't something tangible. It didn't make sense to be named a thing, an idea or a destination because it was a process with no real end. What I thought were failures in my past were really my lessons in finding confidence, perseverance and trust in my gut. Now I realize that whether I met my goals or tripped over them doesn't matter because in the big picture I am learning and growing the whole way anyhow.

A new beginning never ends
Its effect goes on and on
Rippling, moving, forever outward
Like a pebble dropped in a pond

Know your success
Cannot be helped
Your gift is who you are

Today's intention is
Tomorrow's journey
Your purpose will take you far

Trust what you know
As always present
More support than what it might seem

Walk as if you are already there
Be open to all you can dream

L. Maynard

What You Can Expect

This process is divided into three phases. As a tree grows from the ground up, your personal journey will too. It's important to not only understand where you are but also where you have been in order to be prepared to face what comes next. In each phase you will be gaining important knowledge to help you overcome future challenges and bring in more of what you want out of life.

In this workbook you will find a detailed guide for your growth experience that brings together your mind, body and spirit. By doing this you will be able to make healthier more meaningful decisions and have a greater knowledge base to solve problems that come up. Your mind is a powerful assessment tool that communicates with your body constantly. Learning how to listen to that dialogue is the key to unlocking your inner wisdom.

Once inside you can then begin to understand your spiritual nature, the creative energy behind all that you are and all that you do. From this inner place you have the power to see what is truly important to you. This makes acting on it less difficult because there is less running around in trial and error circles. You instinctively think bigger which makes the problems that come up seem smaller and more manageable. You also move ahead more efficiently because you are in tune with your needs and take better care of yourself. Overall, the path to the goal naturally becomes more peaceful because you can see more clearly and you are acting on what you know is best for you.

This book will allow you to create your own personal plan toward a goal that is truly meaningful for you. Uncovering that meaningful goal means taking some time to ask yourself what you really want. It may sound like a simple question but when thinking in terms of your inner wisdom it will take some time to verify what is really true for you. If you don't take the time to understand why you want something you may be quick to take steps that lead you in the wrong direction. Self-awareness is really important to creating a meaningful goal and plan.

The program is designed to help you think bigger so that you can be confident in what you decide and have a way to determine what to do next. Each question in the first two sections will lead you to specific information that will be a part of either Your Profile which is where you write down your inner wisdom or Your Action Plan which is where you organize your goal and the things you need to support yourself as you get there. Taking the extra time in the beginning to set up will help you be much more efficient and save a lot of time in the action phase.

What you get out of this work will be up to you and what you put into it. The art of thinking bigger takes some practice in looking at things from a different perspective. Throughout the book I will be introducing key concepts that will help you understand more about your inner self. Deep down you have all the wisdom you need to heal and create a meaningful life. How you see and interact with your everyday world starts with how you perceive yourself and your place in it. Perceptions can either help increase your inner wisdom or keep you clouded in fearful assumptions.

The key concepts in this book will help you navigate those perceptions so that you can explore what makes the most sense for you. Shifting a perception into something realistic and positive can shift how you experience your everyday for the better. Shift a perception on the inside and you change your reality on the outside.

This book is divided into three phases complete with the tools you will need to support your process and a follow up plan with tips to help on those days when things don't go according to plan.

Phase 1:

<u>Your Roots</u>

This phase will explore where your energy is going in your current experience. You will look at 10 major areas of your life to get clear on how you're spending time and explore what you have taken on as responsibilities. You will also look at what is working for you and what is depleting you. This bird's eye view of information will then be used to formulate your Strengths in your Profile and create a base for your Overall Goals in your Action Plan.

Phase 2:

<u>Your Trunk</u>

The second phase will explore what happened in your past and how that has shaped your life as you know it now. You will look at those pivotal times both good and bad that changed you in some way. Since you are here there is evidence that you have succeeded many things and with that gained much knowledge. In looking at your past experiences you will be able to determine what worked and use that knowledge again to move forward. You will also look at negative habits that may have developed which get in the way of change now. Information gathered here will be divided into two sections. Your wisdom and strengths will go into your Profile to be used as a reference point later during tough times. Your negative unproductive habits will go into your Action Plan either as your Intended Goal or as part the internal Supportive Goals necessary to get where you want to go.

Phase 3:

<u>Your Crown</u>

In phase three you put it all together and get going toward your goal. All the background work of organizing what you know about yourself is really going to pay off now because it gives you a clear solid place from which to push off. This self-awareness has just increased your success rate dramatically and saved yourself from wasting time on things that can be avoided by being proactive.

The work here will be about developing a comprehensive plan that addresses your whole self so that you arrive where you really want and that you have the skills and supports to maintain yourself when you get there.

Working with the whole self is to actively engaging the Mind, the Body and the Spirit. This means utilizing what you know, what you are able to do in your reality and what your creative spirit points to for meaningful next steps. You will then put together the tools you will need to meet your goal and support yourself in the process.

When the process is completed you will have:

A solid big picture view of what works and what needs changing in your life.

A comprehensive list of key concepts that will help you to think bigger and provide a new perspective when facing problems that come up.

A **Profile** that outlines your experience based inner wisdom and strengths.

An organized list of **Overall Goals** with an **Internal Mission** that clarifies your motivations.

An **Action Plan** that covers your **Intended Goal** and any **Supportive Goals** that need attention to be successful with what you want.

You will also have a personalized tools that will help keep you on track:

1. A **3D TO DO List** to help navigate daily tasks from the whole person perspective.
2. A **Compass** to show you whether you are moving toward or away from your goal.
3. A **Backup Plan** with specific tips to help when things don't go as expected.
4. **Tips For Tough Times-** a general guide of ideas to help navigate difficult days.

Where Are Your Roots Growing?

Where is your energy going? What feeds you in your current experience? In this section you will be surveying your life to determine what is working and what is not. You have many roots extending from your being with the goal of finding balance and nutrients to support you. Here you have to first see where your roots are growing and then decide if these roots really support you in balanced way or instead are taking necessary nutrients away.

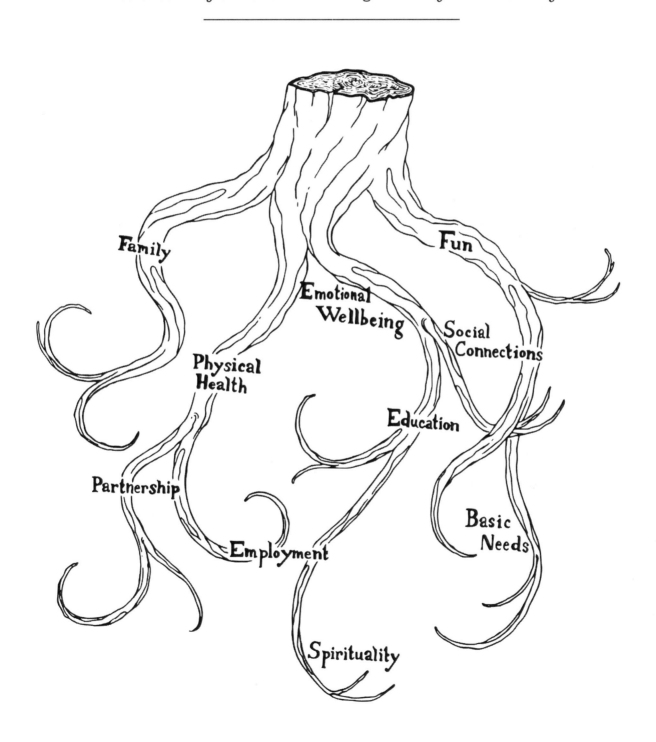

You Are Here

Congratulations! You are in the right place, at the right time. Everything you have experienced so far as led you to this point. You know that change is needed and that awareness means you are listening to your inner wisdom and you are ready to take the next important step.

Coming to this point means that somewhere in your being you have been asking for help. It might be in your thoughts that point to wanting something else. It could also be a physical pain in your body or discomforts you experience with your emotions. However you got here, you most certainly have concluded that you've had enough of your current experience and your body is telling you so too. In looking for personal change you can be confident that you do have the capacity to find the answer. The brain cannot form a question without having a good amount of information behind it. Without that data the brain couldn't put the words together to describe any of what you want. Be assured that if you are asking it means you are tapping into your inner sense of what you need and that inner knowledge will lead you to how to get there.

Before you begin on this path toward making change it's important to teach your brain to think bigger so you can see beyond the stressors you will inevitably face as you go. We all get caught in habits of thinking that make can us feel stuck in certain areas. Stretching yourself to see from a new perspective is at the heart of making a lasting change.

A good place to start practicing how to think bigger is in looking at how you define yourself. How would you fill in this statement?

I am_____.

You might use your name, a job title or your role in your family. You could also describe yourself physically or use a feeling word. You might even give yourself a nick name based on your habits or things you don't like about yourself. Whatever words you put in that statement can never fully define you. Stretching your definition of yourself gives you the freedom to let go of attachments that hold your thinking back. This broader perspective opens up to more tools you can use to problem solve and more creative energy to put toward what you really want.

Key Concept # 1

Who I really am is more than I can see

No matter what has happened to you or how you have responded to it so far, you have not lost who you really are. At the core you are a creative being. The evolving wise one behind all that you know of yourself.

Who you really are is not your situation. That is an external happening which you are having a reaction to. Who you really are is not your emotions or your behaviors either. These are outward expressions that come from within the body and interface with your external environment. Who you really are is not even your thoughts. Behind them is your self-awareness that interprets what they mean. If you can say "I feel terrible," or ask why you think a thought, there is a part of you that is behind all that observing. If you know that you are observing yourself, then you are connecting to the creative part of yourself that is closer to who you really are.

To take that concept a step further you might go on to say that "If I know I am observing myself then what's behind that noticing me observing?" This kind of awareness is where we step into the unknown. There are no words to fully define things here. These kinds of questions can go on infinitely so for now the best you can do is know that there is more to you than what there might seem in this moment. With that, if there is anything in your experience that does not reflect the person you are you can move toward making it different.

Key Concept # 2

Deep down I know how to connect with my true self

While you can't specifically define who you really are, you can find proof that who you are is real when you feel connected to that part of yourself.

To be the creative being you are requires certain elements. Like trees need sunlight and water you will need openness and loving energy in order to grow. When you feel good, you are open and more connected to that creative energy that is you evolving. Any emotion that reflects a sense of joy, peacefulness or fulfillment can be described as a loving one.

When you experience them your thoughts and actions match your need to grow and expand. You naturally think bigger, you have the energy to do more and have the capacity for more contentment in the process.

When you don't feel good you are distracted from who you really are. You are so caught up in handling the stress of a current experience that you have forgotten how to be that creative force behind what's happening. Fear based emotions are the opposite of loving ones and typically bring on stress, anger or sadness. You feel stuck and uncomfortable because this is not your natural state. This is not your fault. It's your biology. The survival instinct you need to navigate this chaotic world. Since the brain can't create and be in survival mode at the same time you will know where you are when you tune into how you feel.

Key Concept # 3

I am not as stuck as I may think I am

As difficult as things might seem at times, it is impossible for you to get so stuck that you can't grow. Even when you are afraid you still have the capacity to choose your focus and reaction. Creativity still exists at your core because again who you really are in not your situation. Your choices may be limited by your situation but deep down your true self still exists and can be acted on.

We can see proof of this in modern science though the study of physics. When technology allowed us to probe the smallest form of matter, we discovered that atoms are divided even further into even smaller bits of matter called particles. We then learned that particles are all essentially made of the same basic elements. What makes then different from one another is that they move at different rates of speed, which are different levels of vibration. In short, what makes a table different from you and I is not different elements but rather the different movement of its particles.

Everything in the known universe comes down to movement. Deep down you are always moving and therefore always evolving. At this very moment you are losing and creating new taste buds, skin cells and bone tissue. Since birth you have been expanding your mind with new information and shifting your perceptions as you have aged. You are literally not the same person you were yesterday. With that in mind, every day provides a new opportunity for your growth.

Key Concept # 4

Once I start momentum will keep me going

Knowing that everything is vibrating means that you too are fundamentally on the move. If you are moving then so too is what you are going through. This road through making change isn't always easy, especially not at first. If you find that you are lacking courage remember that once you begin you will build momentum over time and the ride will go more smoothly. It has to because the laws of physics state that an object in motion tends to stay in motion.

As you move along you will learn many fundamental lessons about yourself. Be confident that once a lesson is learned you cannot unlearn it. You may fall down for a period of time but you won't go back to exactly where you were before. Your evolving self will not allow that.

Exploring Your Roots

Roots are the foundation of where you are putting your energy and what you are receiving back. Just like trees need a balance of nutrients we need a balance of giving and receiving. Understanding how that is currently working for you will tell you what you need to know to move forward.

My Signal for Change:

In this worksheet we are looking to explore what your true motivation is. On the surface it may look a certain way but underneath there may be other reasons for what you want. Understanding them fully will help later as you develop your Internal Mission in your Action Plan. It can also help to keep you keep going in your Back Up Plan if things get difficult.

Assessing your Roots:

In the Root Worksheets you will explore 10 major areas of your life. You are looking for the things that go well and where you might be out of balance. Fill in the sheets as fully as you can. The more information you include here the more you will have to work with later. In many areas you may find that the answers are not concrete as a yes or no. For that fill in both sides as best you can. If you find that you can't fill in something try to fill in the other questions around it. No matter what is going on for you there should be something to say in each life area. To help you fill in the assessment at the bottom of each Root Worksheet you can use the following definitions.

Balanced Roots- These are those areas that are going well. Even though you may not want to focus on this as a goal it's important to know what makes it work. This information will help formulate your strengths in Your Profile. It will also give you good resources to use in meeting your goal.

Unbalanced Roots-These are the areas that really need your attention, the ones that you would like to change Understanding what is going on here will give you good insight in putting together your Overall Goals and your Action Plan.

In Progress- This means you are working on this area and have a plan in place going forward. It may not be exactly where you want it to be but you are doing all you can for now. This is not going to be a priority for your Intended Goal but may be a candidate for your Supportive Goals if necessary.

My Signal for Change

The starting point to exploring roots is your signal for change. This is the hint your mind, body or spirit has given to tell you it's is time to change something. Understanding what brought you here will help to get things focused and provide valuable information which will be used later to assess your motivators in your Internal Mission

_____

What thoughts or insights make me realize I need to make a change:

_____

_____

_____

_____

_____

_____

Feelings that are coming up around this:

_____

_____

_____

_____

Physical symptoms that cause discomfort in my body:

_____

_____

_____

_____

My Roots
Part 1

Basic Needs
Food, Shelter, Clothing etc.

Am I happy with what I have?

Yes

No

What's working well:

_____
_____
_____
_____
_____
_____
_____

What I need more of:

_____
_____
_____
_____
_____
_____
_____
_____

What I can do:

_____
_____
_____
_____
_____

What I cannot control:

_____
_____
_____
_____
_____

☐ Balanced   ☐ In Progress   ☐ Unbalanced

My Roots
Part 2

Employment

Am I satisfied with my job?

Yes

No

What I like about my work:

_____
_____
_____
_____
_____
_____

What I don't like about my work:

_____
_____
_____
_____
_____
_____
_____

What I can do to make things different:

_____
_____
_____
_____
_____

☐ Balanced   ☐ In Progress   ☐ Unbalanced

My Roots

Part 3

Partnership

How is my primary relationship?

Peaceful

Conflicted

How we work well together:

_____
_____
_____
_____
_____
_____
_____

What doesn't work:

_____
_____
_____
_____
_____
_____
_____

My relationship needs:

_____
_____
_____
_____
_____

How I can help improve things:

_____
_____
_____
_____

☐ Balanced   ☐ In Progress   ☐ Unbalanced

My Roots
Part 4

Spirituality
'What does it all mean?'

Do I feel a sense of purpose?

Yes

No

What's meaningful in my life:

_____
_____
_____
_____
_____
_____
_____

Where I feel dissatisfied:

_____
_____
_____
_____
_____
_____
_____

What a meaningful life looks like to me:

_____
_____
_____
_____
_____

☐ Balanced   ☐ In Progress   ☐ Unbalanced

My Roots

Emotional Wellbeing

Am I taking care of my needs?

Yes

No

How I stay balanced:

_____
_____
_____
_____
_____
_____

What get's in the way:

_____
_____
_____
_____
_____
_____

What I need to do more of:

_____
_____
_____
_____
_____

☐ Balanced   ☐ In Progress   ☐ Unbalanced

My Roots

Physical Health

→ How does my body feel?

↙ Healthy

↘ Unhealthy

How I stay healthy:

_____
_____
_____
_____
_____
_____

What interferes with my health:

_____
_____
_____
_____
_____
_____

What I can do differently:

_____
_____
_____
_____

What I cannot change:

_____
_____
_____
_____

☐ Balanced   ☐ In Progress   ☐ Unbalanced

My Roots

Part 7

Social Connections

How is my social life?

Good

Could be better

What I enjoy:

_____
_____
_____
_____
_____
_____

What prevents connection:

_____
_____
_____
_____
_____
_____

What I want to see happen:

_____
_____
_____
_____
_____

☐ Balanced   ☐ In Progress   ☐ Unbalanced

My Roots

Part 8

Family

Am I feeling connected?

Yes

No

My family strengths:

_____
_____
_____
_____
_____
_____
_____

What creates the distance:

_____
_____
_____
_____
_____
_____
_____

Things I can do to help:

_____
_____
_____
_____

What I cannot control:

_____
_____
_____
_____

☐ Balanced   ☐ In Progress   ☐ Unbalanced

My Roots

Part 9

Education

Is there more I'd like to know?

No

Yes

My Skillset:

_____
_____
_____
_____
_____
_____

What I want to explore:

_____
_____
_____
_____
_____
_____

How I can do that:

_____
_____
_____
_____
_____

☐ Balanced   ☐ In Progress   ☐ Unbalanced

My Roots

Part 10

Fun!

Does my life feel joyful?

Yes

No

What I do for fun:

_____
_____
_____
_____
_____
_____

What a fun life looks like:

_____
_____
_____
_____
_____
_____

How I can create that:

_____
_____
_____
_____

☐ Balanced   ☐ In Progress   ☐ Unbalanced

Your Root Check List:

Here take note of where you are with each life area so you have a quick reference for future use. You may also want to jot down anything that would require your immediate attention.

If you are in any kind of emergency in any area you may need to pause here. Note what you need and skip to the Back Up Plan before going any further. You may also need to use the Tips for Tough Times and seek professional assistance. Once the crisis has passed and things have stabilized you then can continue on.

1.   Basic Needs-

2.   Employment-

3.   Partnership-

4.   Spirituality-

5.   Emotional Wellbeing-

6.   Physical Health-

7.   Social Connections-

8.   Family-

9.   Education-

10.   Fun-

What's In Your Trunk?

What are your life changing events and the feelings behind them? What thoughts or beliefs about yourself, your world, the people in your life or your future did you come away with? Here we assess your personal growth rings to determine what you know is true and what your bigger Learning Curves are.

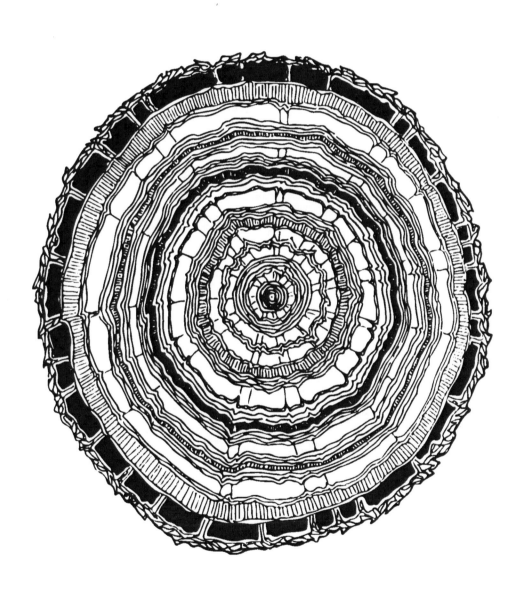

How Did You Get Here?

Your Tree roots extend out to nurture your trunk. Your Trunk then supports your many life changes and takes the brunt of the trauma you've experienced over your lifetime. Physical growth and scars are visible on the outside but the full impact of circumstances is more apparent on the inside. This is where the history of your experience resides and can be seen in the many growth rings. By understanding the lesson in the rings, you can get closer to understanding your wisdom and your true learning curves - the larger life lesson in what you are experiencing.

Great work! You now have a more realistic look at where your energy is rooted so you can see what you want to do different. The next question to explore now is how you got here. Going back for the answers will give you the tools you need to continue to grow. Your arrival to the present has been shaped by your life events and your perception of them. Your perceptions are the meaning you have assigned to the things that have happened. These are unique to you and have impacted not only how you see yourself but also how you see your world and your connection to it.

As you identify your life changing events and the perceptions that accompany them you will also be able to identify the beliefs that came out of them. Your beliefs are what you see as true and they are part of what creates emotional responses in your body. These emotions are the body's reaction to how you see yourself and others. Your beliefs can also influence how you feel about the world and how you respond to life's difficulties.

Understanding this inner world will help you navigate the outer goals you want to achieve. This process of self-discovery is your true Learning Curve. The more you know about yourself the more efficient you can be about getting to your goal. Your past experience is your best resource for your expert wisdom. Any knowledge you have come to know through your experience is yours to keep forever. No one can take that away from you. No future event can change the wisdom you have in your trunk. You may get new information to add to it but you will never lose what is here now. Your wisdom is solid and will support you wherever you chose to go next.

Here are some things to keep in mind as you explore.

Key Concept # 5

My past is the only accurate gauge for my progress

The purpose of this process is to give you a bigger view of yourself by looking over time. You can only truly gauge your progress by looking back on your life. Someone else's life has too many different variables to be an accurate comparison. Even if you share the same life event the results will be different for both of you.

It's also important to remember that your life experience is giving you the perfect skill set you need to take the next step to grow. It's easy to look at someone else's life and pick out what you think is easier or may like better but you are on your own Learning Curve. You have your own momentum set up by what happened in your life previously. The only way change your course is to take your own action based on what you know in that moment.

Comparing yourself to someone else's growth pattern only leads to disappointment because the information they are using is based on their experiences. What they are doing is building skills to grow in the direction they are going. The two can't accurately be compared. All trees grow where they are planted. They can't grow faster than nature will allow and their growth pattern is shaped by where they are rooted. You can't get away from the realty you are rooted in but you can change how you grow from there. The skills you are forming as you go are all that you need to just that.

Key Concept # 6

I am never really alone

Even though we are all on our own Learning Curve we are all interconnected, growing together in the same forest. It can seem isolating at times to go through the stressful trials of living. In those moments try to remember that at the very core we are all made of the same stuff as the universe at large. When we look down into the particles we are made of and the movement they create it becomes clear that your movement can't be separated from the person next to you. At that level we are mingling all the time. Even the smallest action or reaction has impact on those around you. In turn their response to your action has impact on those around them. This goes on infinitely.

Just as you are learning skills from the events in your life others around you are learning by your example. What may present as a negative experience could turn into a positive lesson for both you. We see evidence of this all the time. Have you ever have met someone in a good mood and felt better just standing next to them? How about a smile from a stranger that lifted you on a bad day? Have you ever experienced or even just witnessed a random act of kindness that warmed your heart? You have the opportunity to give and receive these kinds of energetic boosts in any given moment.

Being the evolving person you are can't help but have influence.

You are a very powerful force. As you look into your past try not to let guilt or negative feelings cloud what you have learned. Growing is hard for all of us. Decisions you made in the past were based on what you knew at the time. There was no way to know what you might know now so too much focus on that will keep you from moving forward.

In phase 3 we will talk more about how to foster more positive energy and let go of fear based thinking that promotes a negative impact on yourself. For now just remember that you are not really ever alone and that your experience of growing is very important to you and those around you.

Opening Your Trunk

Everything you have been through has lead you to here, ready for change. Now it's time to put together what have you learned. First you will identify what skills and supports can you take with you on your next goal. Then you will need to get clear about habits might be getting in the way of your success.

Please read the instructions before starting. The worksheets in this phase are designed to help you organize your experience into categories that best suit the path to your goals. It may be helpful to also have a separate notebook or a journal for notes. Use it to consider your thoughts and feelings before filling in the charts. Use it as well to write about additional experiences if you have more than the workbook space allows.

Your Learning Curves:

As you sift through the questions that help to explore your past experiences remember that there are no wrong answers. This is your assessment of what you learned from your experience. As a tree has growth rings to show progress, you have Learning Curves in those emotionally charged experiences that taught you about yourself. Understanding those pivotal moments and how they have impacted you can help you identify what your Learning Curves are and shed light on what you need to do next.

Whether it was a brief moment or a long process, all events have played a part in shaping your life. These big or small pivotal points changed the way you saw yourself, your situation or maybe even your perception of the world. These new insights may have also changed how you think, feel and behave. Look across your whole life span and see what stands out in your Life Roots. Even things that feel insignificant can have meaning if they are showing up in your memory. Not all questions will have specific answers. Be patient with yourself. This is just a way to explore how you see yourself and your world. The right answers are the ones that are meaningful to you.

It is very important to listen to how you are feeling. If you are thinking about an event that still triggers a painful emotional response you can try using The Tips for Tough Times to work with it. If that does not give you relief or your feelings become difficult to manage in your everyday experience then you have not completed the process work needed for this area. It's important to pause and get professional counsel to help you on ways to work through your pain.

What's in Your Trunk:

My Learning Curve- In this box give your life experience or event a title. A word, a sentence or a short paragraph that sums up what you are exploring. Specify whether this is a moment in time or maybe something that took years to get through.

Positive Changes- These are helpful and positive ways that you are different because of what you went through. This is the stuff that you learned that now supports you in some way. Focus on thoughts, feelings or the way you see things differently now. Things you do differently will be placed in the Habit boxes. This information will be used to help create your wisdom in Your Profile.

New Challenges- These are the negative effects of what you went through that now present a new challenge in your life. You may have certain fears you didn't have before. You may have acquired a way of thinking that holds you back. You may also have a physical or emotional injury that you now have to cope with. This information will be used to help identify what you may want to work on as a goal later.

Healthy Habits- These are the things that you do that you didn't before your experience. Focus on the good things that have a positive impact on your life. Don't forget to include the habits you have now that may not be enjoyable. As long as they are healthy it's good to note them.

Unhealthy Habits- These are the things you do that get in the way of progress. New behaviors that distract you or keep you in an unbalanced way of living. Some of these habits have served as coping strategies in the beginning but now are sabotaging your efforts to grow and change. Be as honest as you can and later focusing on this within your action plan will help you get to your goal faster.

What helped me get through this- Here you honor those people or things that supported you along the way. This information is very important to remember in both Your Profile and Your Action Plan

My Trunk

Part 1

My Learning Curve:
An experience that changed me

_____
_____
_____
_____

How my Thoughts Feelings or Actions are different now:

Positive Changes:

_____
_____
_____
_____
_____
_____

New Challenges:

_____
_____
_____
_____
_____
_____

Healthy Habits:

_____
_____
_____
_____

Unhealthy Habits:

_____
_____
_____
_____

What helped me get through this (People, places, programs, books etc..):

_____
_____
_____

My Trunk

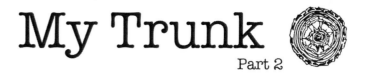

Part 2

My Learning Curve:
An experience that changed me

_____
_____
_____

How my Thoughts Feelings or Actions are different now:

Positive Changes:

_____
_____
_____
_____
_____

New Challenges:

_____
_____
_____
_____
_____

Healthy Habits:

_____
_____
_____
_____

Unhealthy Habits:

_____
_____
_____
_____

What helped me get through this (People, places, programs, books etc..):

_____
_____
_____

My Trunk

Part 3

My Learning Curve:
An experience that changed me

_____
_____
_____

How my Thoughts Feelings or Actions are different now:

Positive Changes:

_____
_____
_____
_____
_____

New Challenges:

_____
_____
_____
_____
_____

Healthy Habits:

_____
_____
_____
_____

Unhealthy Habits:

_____
_____
_____
_____

What helped me get through this (People, places, programs, books etc..):

_____
_____
_____

My Trunk

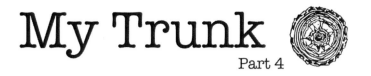

Part 4

My Learning Curve:
An experience that changed me

_____
_____
_____

How my Thoughts Feelings or Actions are different now:

Positive Changes:

_____
_____
_____
_____
_____

New Challenges:

_____
_____
_____
_____
_____

Healthy Habits:

_____
_____
_____
_____
_____

Unhealthy Habits:

_____
_____
_____
_____
_____

What helped me get through this (People, places, programs, books etc..):

_____
_____
_____

My Trunk

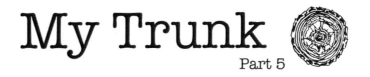

My Learning Curve:
An experience that changed me

_____
_____
_____

How my Thoughts Feelings or Actions are different now:

Positive Changes:

_____
_____
_____
_____
_____

New Challenges:

_____
_____
_____
_____
_____

Healthy Habits:

_____
_____
_____
_____

Unhealthy Habits:

_____
_____
_____
_____

What helped me get through this (People, places, programs, books etc..):

_____
_____
_____

My Trunk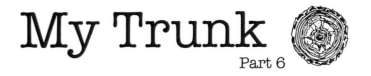

My Learning Curve:
An experience that changed me

_____
_____
_____

How my Thoughts Feelings or Actions are different now:

Positive Changes:

_____
_____
_____
_____
_____

New Challenges:

_____
_____
_____
_____
_____

Healthy Habits:

_____
_____
_____
_____

Unhealthy Habits:

_____
_____
_____
_____

What helped me get through this (People, places, programs, books etc..):

_____
_____
_____

Your Learning Curve Patterns:

In this worksheet you can explore the underlying patterns throughout our experiences. When looking at things from a broader perspective you may find that the same challenges or habits keep coming up in different Life Root areas. These Learning Curve patterns are important because somewhere in your being you are aware that these things need to change and on this deep level you are providing yourself with multiple opportunities to do just that. Remember we are always evolving. This occurs not just physically but emotionally and spiritually as well. Patterns become very important to realize as we move to make change because sometimes they can get in the way. They are most often linked to a core hurt or a basic need. You may also have more than one.

When working with a Learning Curve it is not always a complete circle. It is really more like a spiral. It's possible to have an understanding about yourself in one Life Root area but still be struggling with it in another. It doesn't mean you have failed, you have just come around for another loop and will spiral forward again as you deepen your understanding in this other area too.

Once you have completed these Learning Curve questions you are finished with the background work of setting up your Action Plan. The positive things you have gained from your experiences will have a place in your Profile. The things you are still working on will then go into the Overall Goals for your Action Plan.

By taking the time to do this background work you are going to be better able to plan and take action that accomplishes not only your goal is but also takes care of what you need to reach that goal. Not doing this step could lead to confusion and may keep you from getting where you really want to go.

An Important Warning:

Learning Curves are very difficult to see clearly when you are in the middle of developing them. It takes time to forge a growth ring in a tree and they cannot be understood until after the fact when they become that visible circular memory. Remember to check in with how you are feeling, use the Tips For Tough Times for support, and if needed seek professional help. Taking the time that you need now to sort out that will help you get to your goal much faster.

If you try to move ahead without addressing what you need to these emotions will come back and can prevent you from making the right decisions in your action plan. This doesn't mean you are failing at your process but rather that you are strengthening it. Taking time to understand emotional pain will not only give way to new insight and clarity about your direction, but also provide a more solid foundation to maintain your goal once you get there.

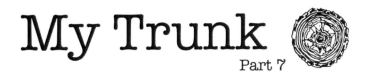
My Learning Curve Patterns:

Similar situations that keep repeating in my life:

_____
_____
_____
_____

Thought patterns that keep me stuck:

_____
_____
_____
_____

Chronic feelings that confuse my progress:

_____
_____
_____
_____

Things I do regularly that hold me back:

_____
_____
_____
_____

My Profile

This is where you will put all the wisdom you have learned from your past.
It will serve as a reminder of your progress and a resource during tough times.
As you fill the information in the appropriate place feel free to be creative.
Fun colors, pictures, drawings or special quotes are a nice addition.

It is important to recognize where you are right now. You have finished gathering information and will be getting ready to make it all work for you. To do that you must first step into what is true for you right now. When you are operating from what is true it will create a path that is much clearer, goes smoother and allows peacefulness to come in. Following your truth is being in alignment with your whole self. Your mind connects with what your body is feeling and your experience then evolves from a place of meaning. If in the future you are not feeling well reset back here with all that you know. Even in the worst of experiences this information will stay solid and can carry you through.

Filling in your Profile:

Things you have survived- When completing Profile pages 1 and 2 remember the things that happen in your life always have the ability to teach you something helpful. The goal here is to take the experiences you wrote about and translate them into a concentrated bit of wisdom that you can call on in the present day. When you do this you are having the direct experience of being aligned with all three key parts of yourself. Your mind, body and sense of meaning come together and everything makes sense. Even if it's only for a second when you tap in like that you know who you are that will point you to what is naturally next for you. Even if the wisdom is not something you are fully living right now that's okay. Your wisdom is meant to be a reminder when you forget yourself.

It's a bit like writing poetry so you will need a separate sheet of paper. Look at your Trunk notes and pick an event. Note the time frame that it occurred and then work on writing the positive thing you took away from that. The goal is to get to the deepest wisdom possible. Generally, we start with what is on the surface, our initial thoughts and emotions. I encourage you not to stop there. Even though all that you are putting together is absolutely true there may be more to understand underneath that. The deeper you can go the more solid it will feel.

If you start with your initial thought then ask how you feel about that thought. If you have a feeling then ask yourself what that feeling is trying to tell you about yourself. You will know it is right when it feels good and has a powerful meaning. Make sure to write your statement in the present tense with the fewest words possible. It should also be packed with conviction. I AM _____I CAN_____I KNOW_____ or I FEEL_____ are great places to start. Be patient and wait until you feel your thoughts, your emotions and your sense of meaning all combine. If you can't feel the power behind the words keep asking more questions and the right words will come.

Some Examples:

When I was growing up I was surrounded by people who would criticize and ignore what I had to say. With that I came to believe that what I had to say was not important. I then isolated myself and carried the feeling of being invisible throughout most of my life. Years later when I was learning how to meditate a thought came through my mind:

"If you want to be visible to others you first have to be visible to yourself"

I knew what my thought meant logically but in that moment I didn't feel it fully. I was still feeling invisible so it became my goal to change that. Now as I look back and put together what I learned I can see that my thought was in response to my fear based feeling of being unimportant. It was a positive idea but more of directive and not a reflection of who I am. Now years later I can think with a feeling of conviction that what I say does matter. It matters so much I had to write it down. Putting it to words has helped me realize that I am not invisible and that feels very powerful. It would seem like I can stop here at "I am not invisible" and let that be my wisdom but if I really dig I have to acknowledge that who I really am is not about what I am not. Who I really am is visible. Stated in present tense and with fewer words:

"I AM VISIBLE!"

I once worked with someone who almost lost a child due to a medical condition. She was faced with a decision about his treatment that had no guarantee of success. In order for her to decide she had to be ready to let him go completely. The first wisdom she thought was that the ordeal taught her a lot about how grateful she was for her children. She also felt that she had a strength and stamina that she didn't know she had prior to that. While all of this was true when she read it back to me I didn't feel any conviction. Her tone fell flat because she was only reflecting the top layers of thought and emotion. Looking deeper she learned that after facing her worst nightmare as a parent she is now able to manage daily family stressors without fear.

Nothing in her stressful life was as bad as facing death of her son. With that her wisdom changed from "I have the strength to push through anything" with a matter of fact tone to a very enthusiastic:

"I AM FREE!"

Another case example involved a young man looking for what he could have possibly gained from being bullied as a teenager. Initially he was only able to identify the negative impact, which was distrusting people and trying to control everything. As a child he ended up in the role of the victim because he felt that the situation was out of his control. Over time he thought that to prevent that feeling from ever happening again he had to push through situations and manipulate people to get his needs met. As we explored this he came up with the connection that as long as he was in control he couldn't be overpowered. "I am not a victim" was his first wisdom. While this statement is true and could have stood on its own I felt that it was incomplete. Looking deeper he was able to see that if he is not a victim then he didn't have to waste energy trying to control others. He could take his power back and focus it on the one person he did have control of. In the end he was able to firmly say:

"I AM IN CONTROL OF MYSELF AND MY CHOICES!"

The bottom line here is to write something that when spoken out loud feels powerful, supportive and meaningful. If you need other examples you can explore any of the key concepts in this book. Each of those were my bits of wisdom after years of study and exploring many of my own life experiences.

Expressing your true self- This is how you act on what is within you. The things that you do that represent who you really are as a loving creative being. Make notes that remind you of what you are doing when you feel happy and centered.

Finding gratitude- It's important to note here that you focus on what you really appreciate. This is not where you write what other people think you should be grateful for; this is your list so be personal and specific. Don't forget the little things as well (favorite foods, movies, sports places in nature, colors, textures, modern conveniences, fun activities, music, etc.).

How you influence others- This is a reminder of how powerful you really are. We all have the ability to affect others every day. Even small exchanges between total strangers can have a big impact. Explore how you positively impact others. These can be big gestures or everyday things. Think about acts of kindness, how you communicate or greet people. Think about what kind of example you are to others. Look at how you express your true self and note how that might influence others. Even simple things others witness can be very powerful. A smile, a hug, enjoying your work or a sense of style that matches you can all have influence. Sometimes doing nothing but being a calm presence or an example of professionalism can be enough. Be broad and consider the things you might take for granted and not notice about yourself. If you are not sure ask someone else what they see in you.

Things you do well- Don't be afraid to be truly honest here. You have come very far through a number of things. List your strengths that have developed and carried you through to now.

Things that are going well- Review your Balanced Roots and note the things that are going smoothly in your life.

What reminds you of who you really are- This is where you acknowledge the things outside of yourself that reflect who you really are. Remember in order to put language to something you have to an internal reference point for what it is. When you encounter something beautiful, someone who brings a smile to your face or a place that brings you peace, you are connecting an external experience to a part of the love and peacefulness that is already inside you. Note what, where or with whom you feel the most happy or peaceful. Take a look at who or what in your community influences you.

Notes to self- These are your most productive or positive thoughts, the ones you may forget when you are having a bad day. It could be a quote, a song lyric, a picture, something someone said to you or wisdom you have come to through in your own experience. You can also be creative and write a letter to yourself from a future-self depicting what it will be like once this bad time is over. However you want to approach this only has to make sense to you. Be your own coach and talk yourself up.

What Happened:

_____
_____

When: _____

My Wisdom: _____
_____
_____
_____
_____

I

AM

STRONGER

&

WISER

with each life

experience

What Happened:

_____
_____

When: _____

My Wisdom: _____
_____
_____
_____
_____

My Profile

What Happened:

_____
_____

When: _____

My Wisdom: _____
_____
_____
_____

My
truth
is
a

What Happened:

_____
_____
When:_____
My Wisdom:_____
_____
_____
_____
_____
_____

What Happened:

_____
_____
When:_____
My Wisdom:_____
_____
_____
_____
_____
_____
_____

solid
support

What Happened:

_____
_____
When:_____
My Wisdom:_____
_____
_____
_____
_____
_____
_____

no
matter
what
happens
next

I express my true self
when I...

_____
_____
_____
_____
_____
_____
_____
_____

I am grateful
for...

_____
_____
_____
_____
_____
_____
_____
_____

_____
_____
_____
_____
_____
_____
_____
_____

I influence
others by...

Things I do
well...

Things that are
going well...

Things that
remind me of
who I really am...

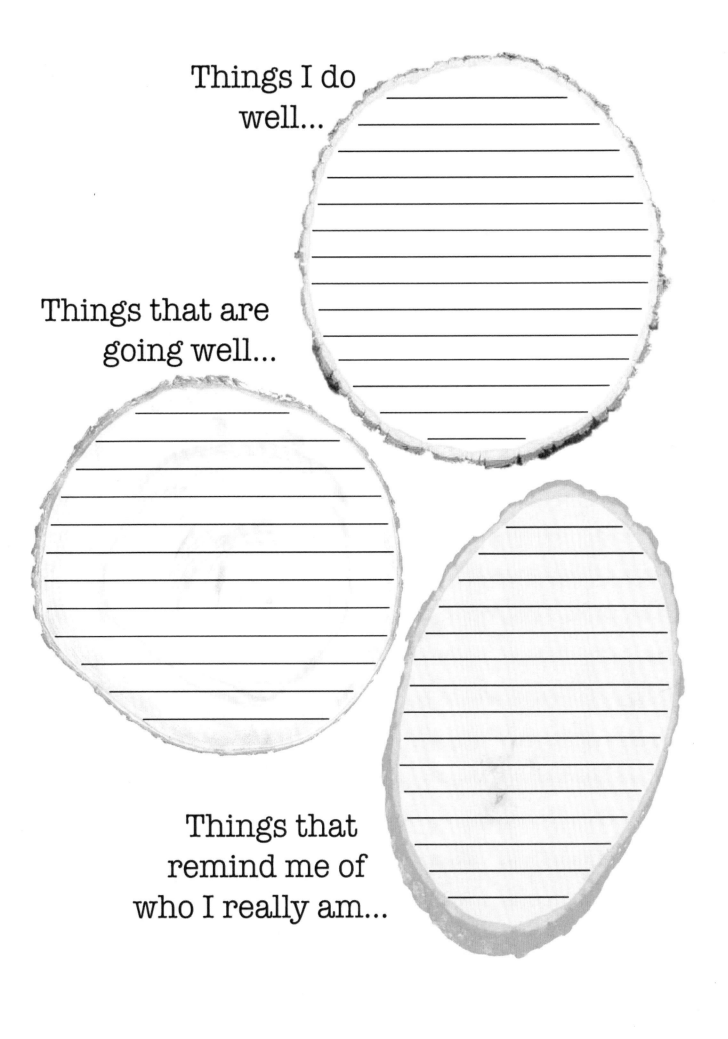

Notes...

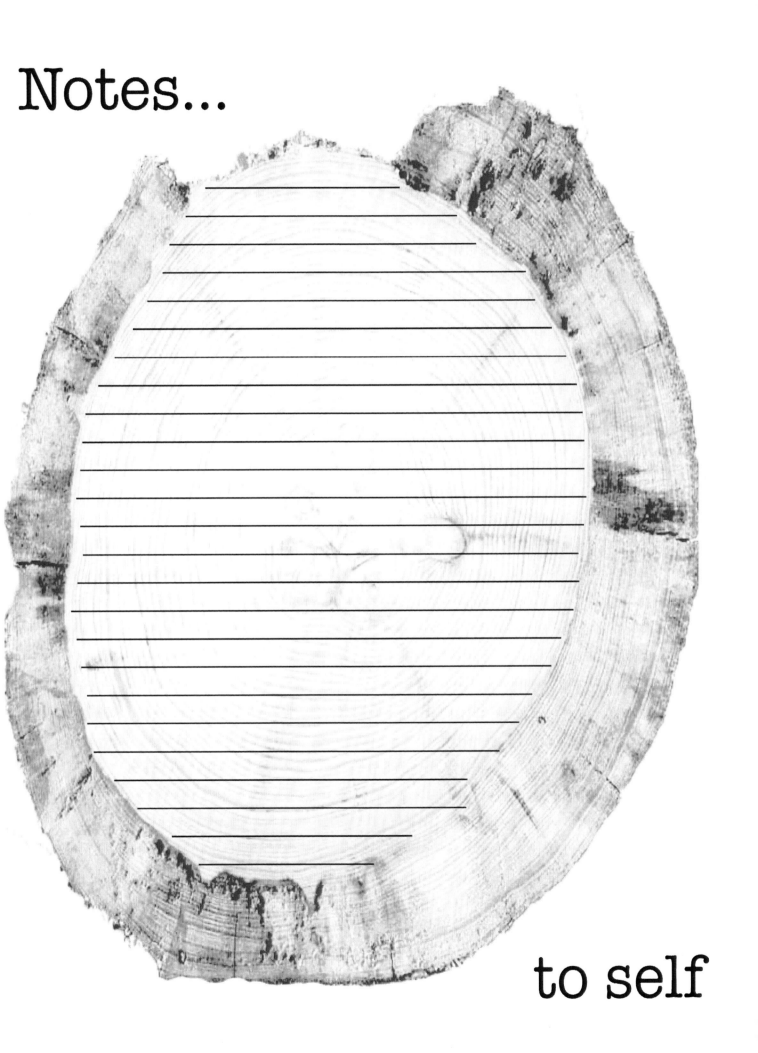

to self

What's on Your Tree Crown?

What do you want in your life and how are you making that happen? Here we look at you in the moment of moving forward. How do you want to express yourself? Do you have colored leaves or needles? What direction do you want to grow in? How tall do you want to grow? Are you ready to accept your growth and take charge of building on it?

———————————————————

Where Do You Want To Grow Now?

Now that you know where your Roots are going and what your Learning Curves are you can better develop a practical Action Plan that supports the kind of life you want to create. You have now grown into your Crown. Like a tree in the sunlight this is where you are most visible. This is where you get to express yourself in the moment, where you can breathe in what the world has to offer and decide how you want to respond.

Welcome back to the present! You have done well understanding what you have been through and can now make it work for you. Growing into your Crown is the act of following your path. This is the process of living, where you get to be creative about how you express yourself. There is no end result here. Just as a tree never stops growing you will not either.

The Action Plan will focus on one goal you choose as a priority. Once completed you can go back and create a new plan for a new goal. You can circle through as many times as you want.

As you reach your goals you will find contentment for a while but over time new desires will arise. It is the human condition. It's how we evolve and grow.

In the process of growing you will have some basic elements with which you have to contend. Just as trees grow where they are planted you too come from the reality in which you were born. For some of us this presents a challenge, yet as a tree will grow into strange forms to stay connected to the sun, you too can stretch and find your way to stay open to love and peace. Remember being open is how you connect to who you really are. This is not some foreign wishful place of unicorns and rainbows but rather a state of being. It is a thought, a feeling or a quiet knowing within your spirit that you have the capacity to realize in any given moment. I know it will sound impossible at times but with a solid plan, support and practice this can be a very real part of your experience.

A couple more Key Concepts before you get started:

Key Concept # 7

My success is in the process not the goal

Now that you are ready for action it can be easy to lose sight of what is really important. You have always been and will continue to be on a journey. Goals are great but true happiness can never be found in something intended in the future. The function of a goal is to give you a focus. It provides a direction to put your energy. If you put off being happy until the goal arrives you may have a long time to wait. Also what will happen if the goal is not possible in the way you first thought and has to change? What if you decide to do something different? If you put too much expectation in the outcome of what you want then your joy will continually be ahead of you. Try to think bigger than the goal and include where you are today in getting there because too strong an expectation on the end can also get in the way of the creative process itself. If you are too focused on one particular outcome what you want could show up in a way you might not recognize and you could miss out.

There is some very exciting stuff happening right now. Look at what you had to move through to get here. Notice what it feels like right now planning to forge ahead in such a meaningful way. Try and feel the wonder of new ideas and experiences as they occur. This rush of movement in your plan is where the action really is. This is your reality, a journey and all this work will bring your goal to you. Accepting that is to grow forward and find peace in the knowledge that what is meant to be next will come. When it's time for your goal it will be so much more fun because in real time you can then have a real feeling and a real celebration about it.

Key Concept # 8

I am powerful

When you express the desire to change you are taking an inner motivation and beginning to make it move into the outer world. In this process of getting things started your words are very important. What you say to yourself and others has impact. We see this when we look at the mind-body connection. Every thought you have creates a physical response in the body. Just like a computer monitor will show everything you type on the keyboard, the brain automatically translates whatever you say. The translation becomes chemicals released from the brain to create emotional reactions. In this way words become very powerful.

Emotions have an energetic charge. This extends from you to impacts others and your environment. We all have this ripple effect. The energy you release will pair up with similar energy because like attracts like. You can see evidence of this by the way people respond to you and how you interpret what's going on around you. You will notice that on a bad day everything seems to go wrong yet on a good day things seem to fall right into place. This is no accident. We are constantly co-creating our experience and how you live within that is how you interpret it. In your inner world it is all up to you.

Owning Your Crown

Here you decide what you want to bring into your life and how you are planning to do it. This is the last step before taking action. You have done well with the work of establishing where you are and deciding what you want. You have been successful in getting through your past to here and so now feel confident that you have all that you need to keep moving toward what you want.

Organizing what you want in your life:

Your Overall Goals:

This is your master list of things you want to do in your life. Go back and review your Roots. What areas are not balanced the way you would like? In each of those areas review what you want to be different. Sometimes it is hard to know what you are asking. If it's helpful, look at what you don't want in this area and take the opposite to be what you do want.

You have two categories here.

1 Things to do- are those tangible actions you would like to take. Be sure to cover all Unbalanced or In Progress Roots for possible ideas. Include everything and don't worry about this list being too big. You want to have it all down so you are not wasting time thinking about trying to remember things. Use an extra notebook if needed.

2 Supportive needs- are those things you need to do to support the action steps you are planning. These might be things around taking care of yourself, building confidence or even developing a new skill necessary to meet your goal. Take another look at your Learning Curves. Are there any sabotaging thoughts, feelings or habits that needs to be addressed?

Identifying your Inner Mission:

Review your Overall Goal List and choose your top priority. Be specific about what you want and why. Check your Signal to Change page to add clarification to your motivation. Also take the time to really visualize what it will look like to achieve what you want. This is very important because if you can really see it you have a much better chance to fully realize it. This section is the base from which all of your thoughts, feelings and actions will stem from while you are working on your goal. If you forget what you are doing and why, this is where you can reset. If you decide to change your goal, come back here and make sure your mission is lined up properly and then continue on with new action steps.

Developing Your Action Plan:

Formulating your Intended Goal:

As you move forward in creating your mission you will need to generate language that keeps you heading in the right direction. It's important that what you say to yourself doesn't sabotage what you are trying to do.

If you use future tense words like someday I will_____, or I hope I can_____, you are giving the brain a directive to ponder these ideas rather than act on them. Having these kinds of thoughts is a good beginning to look at what you want but doesn't give the brain any awareness that these are ideas you are ready to act on.

If you say to yourself I want_____, or I wish_____, you are giving your mind a direct order to create a state of feeling wishful or wanting. In your mind's eye the work is done. You asked to want something so there you go. Now you have the feeling of wanting.

Intentions are not merely thoughts or feelings they are intended action. When you formulate them they are written in the present or in the form of action steps. I am in the process of_____. I will_____. I am doing or being_____. I understand that this is a play on words but it becomes very important in the mind-body connection.

If you want to really get going you have to give the brain a directive to wake up and take action. Even if you don't know what to do, asking a question will fire the creative energy in the brain to go looking. That is much better than telling it to sit still.

Another important factor is how you feel about what you are intending. Saying the words to yourself is one step toward getting the ball rolling. Next is the feeling that those words evoke. This is what determines whether you are moving forward with your goal or being held back. If you feel confident about what you are saying, odds are you will have more success in completing your goal. If you doubt that what you are asking for can happen, you are sending a mixed message to your brain and then on to your body. Mixed messages cancel each other out. They are opposing thoughts that keep the mind and body going in a kind of circular pattern that keeps you stuck.

How to accomplish your Intended Goal:

This is your specific list of things to do that focus on your Intended Goal. Be sure to include short and long term steps with a timeline. You could start with immediate tasks and then work out from there but don't worry too much about the order of things here. You will organize daily and weekly tasks next in your 3D TO DO List.

Identifying Supportive Needs:

Review your Supportive Needs with your Intended Goal in mind. You will want to focus on those that are directly necessary to complete your goal. Others that may be there can be worked on later. You can't truly respond to all the things you want to change at the same time. The good news is that when it comes to working with the whole-self you can work hard in one area and feel the benefit of improvement across the others as well. Change your thinking and your body responds differently. Change your emotional wellbeing and your sense of purpose grows. No matter where you start you are going to change as a whole person.

If a Supportive Need is taking up all of your energy and preventing you from moving toward your Intended Goal it may be that you need to fully address that Supportive Need first. Transfer it to Your Intended Goal and then develop your plan again from there. With that in place your Supportive Needs will be about addressing any barriers that block that need from getting met. This may require outside counsel or coaching and that's okay. Once you have addressed that need you can resume efforts toward your original Intended Goal.

My Crown

Part 1

Overall Goals

Things to do:

_____
_____
_____
_____
_____
_____
_____
_____
_____
_____
_____
_____
_____
_____
_____
_____
_____
_____
_____
_____
_____
_____
_____
_____

Supportive needs:

_____
_____
_____
_____
_____
_____
_____
_____
_____
_____
_____
_____
_____
_____
_____
_____
_____
_____
_____
_____
_____
_____
_____
_____

My Crown

Part 2

My Inner Mission:

What I want now:

_____

_____

_____

Why I want to do this:

_____

_____

_____

_____

_____

_____

_____

_____

What it looks like when I make this happen:

_____

_____

_____

_____

_____

_____

_____

_____

_____

My Action Plan:

My intended goal:

_____

_____

_____

Things to do to accomplish my goal:

_____   _____
_____   _____
_____   _____
_____   _____
_____   _____
_____   _____
_____   _____
_____   _____
_____   _____
_____   _____
_____   _____
_____   _____
_____   _____

Supportive needs to keep me focused:

_____

_____

_____

_____

_____

Keeping Yourself On Track

This is where we really bring your whole-self into the work. A plan is just a plan until you put it into action. Making sure your actions address both your goal and your internal needs will not only get you where you want faster it will make the journey there go much smoother.

Staying focused and motivated with even a well-organized plan can be difficult without support. Things will not always go perfectly. They can't because growth is an organic process that is by nature unpredictable and messy at times. These times are not failures they are growth spurts that provide new information and opportunity. Knowing that this is inevitable it's important to take time developing a guide to help you push through those difficult times.

In this section you will create the following personalized set of tools that will help you stay aware, organized and supported no matter what might happen.

Your 3D To Do List:

This is where you break down your Action Plan into daily or weekly tasks. The categories listed will help you identify and cover all parts of yourself. By working each day from a whole person perspective you are taking better care of yourself as you move toward what you want. This will ease the process of getting there and help you stay grounded so when you get to your goal you will have the skills and strength to maintain yourself. If you only focus on the goal you will miss important needs that could waste time by taking you off track, or worse, keep you from getting to your goal at all.

Your Compass:

This is a tool to help you quickly assess whether you are moving toward your goal or getting stuck in a negative pattern. Here you will insert your thoughts, feeling and actions into a grid that will map out what personally works for you and what might be sabotaging your efforts. Being honest about what you think, feel and do when under stress can give you good insight into how to get around a tough situation. Also, focusing on what works well will get you to your goal quicker.

Your Backup Plan:

This is the alternative plan for when things don't go as expected. Even well made plans get interrupted by life. Health problems, traumatic events, unpredictable people or just a plain bad mood can sometimes bring things to a complete halt. Here you can think ahead and give yourself some ideas about what to do. This will be your self-reference on a bad day. Even here no plan is a guarantee. If you are not able to pick yourself back up there are additional ideas in the Tips for Tough Times section. If this doesn't work seek out other supports outside of this process. Before you get into the practical steps of what to do here are a few final key concepts to help your inner self as you go.

Key Concept # 9

I am whole

Whether you are conscious of it or not your mind, body and spirit are always working together. Thoughts are generated in the mind as a way to understand our internal world or external environment. Underneath thoughts is your spirit. This is the part of you that carries your beliefs and the meaning you create out of your experiences. Both are wrapped up in your body that supports you through your life's journey. What happens with one will affect the other two.

Learning to listen to each part of yourself can be helpful in navigating life and making change. We receive information constantly on all levels. We can't pay attention to it all so we have filters to weed through what comes in. In the weeding process some things get thrown out, some things automatically get filed in our unconsciousness and the rest we deal with. The information that we are aware of then gets filtered consciously. Here we decide what we focus on. If we are not careful we may throw out vital information.

When it comes time to make a change the first information you receive is through your spirit. It's that quiet intuitive voice in your head or that smoldering gut feeling in your body. It's the signal most of us ignore at first. Once the spirit gives up trying to talk to you the mind takes over and translates that nagging need to change into your emotions. Once the signal hits here you start to have feelings about wanting to change. You may feel sad, irritable or dissatisfied. In general, whatever emotion you experience will not feel good. If you ignore this signal it will eventually come out in your physical body. Distress over time will come to equal physical pain in some way. The more you ignore your body's efforts to communicate the worse you will physically feel.

While you are working to be more aware of your mind, body and spirit as we go through this process feel confident that you don't have to be perfect at it. Doing work in even just one area will positively affect the others. It has to because in order for you to be born into this journey called life the mind, the body and the spirit needed to come together simultaneously. To be alive means that all parts of you are still intact and working together.

Key Concept # 10

I am part of something bigger

Life can be overwhelming at times as you move through your day but rest assured there is a bigger picture at work here. Your situation is one of many you have had and will have in your lifetime. Remember you have a bigger Learning Curve. It may be hard to see why this is happening in this moment but rest assured that it is part of a larger cause and effect pattern that you just don't have a way to grasp yet. If you could step back from this and look at your evolvement as a whole you would see clearly what got you here and what to do next. Be patient and try to realize that your life is more than your current situation. Just because an ant can't see further than the ant hill doesn't mean the larger world doesn't exist. In the same way you don't have to assume you are lost just because things aren't going well in this moment.

It can be hard to keep yourself on track with your goal when you look around and everything is in chaos. When having a bad day and coming from fear, a bigger more loving perspective might be helpful. Try to step back and appreciate the beauty of your own growth pattern. It has taken so much for your Roots connect to your Truck and for your Trunk to support your Crown. That is an impressive creation when you think of all that has gone into living your life. Step back further see how your life pattern connects to others. Your energy has a powerful influence that impacts not only how they connect to other people but also to the world at large. If you could have the distance to see it all clearly it would be a beautiful coordinated pattern.

To the universe our planet is just like an ant hill. From that perspective the everyday chaos doesn't exist. Earth appears as a beautiful mix of color twirling around the sun. What do you think it would be like to step back even further and look at the whole universe? What kind of beautiful colors and movement patterns would you be able to see then?

In the big picture a lot of what we worry about just doesn't matter.

Key Concept # 11

Who I really am is love in motion

In the beginning of this process we looked at love only in terms of emotion. We learned that what feels good is loving and what feels uncomfortable is a version of fear. We now know these feelings cannot be a definition of who we truly are because they are observable when they come into our awareness. We also know that feelings serve as a signal to inform us of whether we are evolving naturally toward a goal or slowing down because of a fearful situation.

Love is just as much about the creative energy behind it as the emotional experience of it. Loving emotions cannot be separated from the evolving energy that sparked them. Remember we are whole. The mind, body and spirit all work together. The difference between a fear based feeling and a loving emotion is the same as everything else. A different rate of speed.

Even when things veer off plan you don't have to lose sight of your true self. All of our experience comes down to perspective and you don't have to travel the universe to see it. If you are feeling bad try looking outside yourself. If you can see something beautiful, loving or funny then you are opening up to those same things that are already inside you. Remember your brain wouldn't recognize it if you didn't already possess that kind of understanding internally.

The external world we perceive is a direct reflection of what we are focusing on internally. If you are feeling afraid or upset that is what you are going to notice in your outer world first. Try looking from a loving perspective. Is there anything you might be grateful for? Even if it's a very small idea it will begin to create a shift in you toward opening to who you really are.

Remember you wouldn't be here if you weren't the creative evolving being you are. You are love in action. You know this is true when you feel it as loving emotions. The fact that you are alive and growing means that fear does not exist at your core. At that level you can only come from love, which connects to the kind of energy that moves forward. If that weren't true you couldn't have evolved this far. You may feel afraid for a while but you won't stay stuck forever. Deep down you know you are always moving. Listen to what your fear has to say, learn from it, and then get back to the loving you. The sooner you embrace that love is what's real for you and fear is just the feeling you get when you forget that fact the sooner you will find happiness again.

Embracing your true self

    is like looking into

        the most beautiful sunset

            and realizing it's your own reflection.

3D To Do List

This a three dimensional way to organize yourself around your Intended Goal. It will give you a well-rounded approach to choosing tasks that help you get closer to what you want. By working with all parts of yourself regularly you will have much better results and be better grounded to maintain your goal when you get there.

How to use your 3D To Do List:

This is a general guide to opening up your focus to include your whole self. This doesn't have to be as overwhelming as it may sound. Even small tasks in each area can create a big change. The important thing here is awareness. See yourself as a whole person who needs all parts for equal footing. Lose track of one for a length of time and you can't help but fall down in some way. Remember you can't change everything at once. Choose manageable tasks for each category that fit your reality.

This worksheet is a format meant to be used over and over. It will easily translate into your planner or anywhere you write your list of things to do. Feel free to make copies of the 3D To Do List page for your personal use.

MIND:

What you think will determine how your body will function and respond to daily demands. Staying focused on your goal and your well-being will help you continue to move forward. If you are not sure how this is going for you, check your Compass and if need be, proceed to the Tips for Tough Times section and look for ideas around shifting stressful or unproductive thoughts.

Things to think about are:

How can I bring my mind in line with what I want? What do I need to learn? What can I say to myself to keep my thoughts productive?

Saying affirmations / positive thinking books / educational books, TV or activities etc.

BODY:

Your body is the vehicle that walks you through life. It is a beautiful multilayer machine that needs your care and respect to function at its best. This can be in terms of providing a healthy lifestyle or respecting the reality you are in. Trying to be someone or somewhere you are not is pulling your body out of alignment with your environment. This creates a lot of stress on your system. You can have a great vision for what you want in your imagination but your body cannot hold that up if it doesn't match what is realistic in your experience. Being honest with yourself and taking honest action is important here and any positive attention you can give your body is very welcomed. This can be in very simple ways that fit into your life style. Small healthy choices can make a big difference in meeting your goal.

Things to think about:

What does my body need to function in my world? What am I doing to take care of my health? How do I address my feelings if needed? What can I do to make what I want tangible?

Healthy eating / movement / face your emotions / be kind to yourself / self-care activities etc.

SPIRIT:

This is remembering why you do things and finding joy in the process. Moving forward without this makes it hard feel grounded and solid in where you are headed. You need to remember and express who you are in order to balance the hard work of change with fun. Taking time to breathe in this way will help rejuvenate your focus and build your stamina. Take time to play with what is meaningful for you. Stay connected with the larger framework of what you are doing. Remembering your Inner Mission will help stay on top of outer goals.

Things to think about:

How can I honor my spirit in the process? What can I do to remember the meaning behind what I am doing? How can I be creative or have fun while still moving forward?

Play / be creative /inspirational activities / visit nature / gratitude / prayer / meditation etc.

HAVE TO'S:

These are the tangibles we can't avoid. Some things on this list will be to meet your goal and others will be to maintain your basic needs and responsibilities. It is important to have some order with your daily basics and your goal, but don't forget that you are a whole person and your self-care needs are important too. Yes, you are moving toward your goal, but you are also living in this moment. Being aware of your whole-self can keep you centered and allow the growth process to be a whole lot more peaceful.

You only have so much energy to put into a day and it's important to mindfully decide where that goes. Your 3DTo Do List doesn't come at you, as it feels sometimes, it comes from within you. In order to stay balanced you need to consider all parts of yourself. It can be in very small ways if time doesn't allow but it still needs to be there to stay present in your process.

Things to think about:

What do I have to do to get through the day or the week? / What needs to happen at home or at work to keep things going? / What am I going to do to work on my goal?

Try to be realistic and not overbook yourself.

3D To Do List

Mind:

_____
_____
_____
_____

Body:

_____
_____
_____
_____

Spirit:

_____
_____
_____
_____

Have to's:

_____
_____
_____
_____

Your Compass

This is the tool you will use to determine where you are and where you need to focus to stay on your path. This is your personal navigation system based on your feelings and your personal responses to stress and joy. This will be the directional that will tell you if you are moving forward or getting stuck in the wrong direction.

What your Compass can do for you:

Your Compass is a way to visually see where your thoughts, feelings and actions are when they are hard to define. This information is very important when it comes to making decisions and working toward a goal because emotions can be a helpful gauge to determine what direction you are moving. For the purpose of our work together I am framing emotions into two categories. I will refer to all those emotions that cause stress, upset or pain as fear based emotions. All others that feel good will be considered love based emotions. There are many nuances of emotion that come into your everyday experience, but for the purpose of this tool a broader perspective of emotion will help you quickly assess and make immediate changes if necessary.

We need our emotions to navigate our daily experience. Fear helps us survive the high stress world in which we live. Love helps us connect with who we really are. Emotions are the body's way of letting us know when we are open to who we are or when we are distracted. Your thoughts and actions will be extensions of the corresponding emotion.

When you are coming from fear you are limited on all levels. Instinct takes over, making your primary goal survival. All thoughts, behaviors and action will then line up with that emotion. Fear tells us when we are in danger or when we are stuck. It is good information to hear. Your fear limits you on purpose so you can concentrate on taking immediate action or plan for a potential threat. When in danger fear can save your life. On the flip side, too much fear when there is no immediate threat of danger can get in the way of meeting a goal. This kind of fear is prolonged emotional distress or worry. It creates fear-based thinking and can develop into the sabotaging of coping habits. We all experience this yet it can be hard to see in ourselves. When you are coming from fear you are unconscious. Your body will not allow you to see the bigger picture because you are concentrating on just getting to the next moment. Your Compass will be your sense of direction when you are unable to read your body's signals.

When you are coming from that loving peaceful side of yourself your thoughts, feelings and actions are no longer bogged down by fear or focused on just survival. You can breathe calmly, you are conscious and can make choices about things beyond the moment. This part of you does not rely on instinct but rather intuitively knows what is best and can make better decisions for you. In this state of being you have the ability to see the bigger picture and tap into your larger self-awareness. You are evolving, not stuck and therefore more connected to who you really are. This state of being can be hard to maintain in our chaotic world. Your Compass can help you stay aware of where you are so you know how to have more peaceful and loving experiences.

How to use your Compass:

In this section list your thoughts in the left column, habits in the right one and feelings down the middle. The horizontal line in the middle separates healthy evolving choices on top from ones that come from survival on the bottom. Once you fill in your information in the appropriate places you will see that they line up under either Love or Fear. Within those two categories are your coinciding thoughts, feelings and actions. In those moments when you can't quite identify your feeling you can look to your thoughts or behaviors to give you a clue. Any thoughts or behaviors you are engaging in that are on the fear side of your Compass will turn you away from reaching your goal. You may want to rethink them and try to think or do something from the opposite love side of your Compass. Take care to be honest with yourself and try not to be judgmental. This will just keep you in fear longer. Fear-based thoughts and behaviors are a signal. Try to listen and act accordingly. Sometimes we need the down time of being stuck. When you are ready to let it go, work toward things on the loving side of your Compass. If you need to you can go to your Backup Plan or the Tips for Tough Times Section to help you change your direction.

You may also find that you do the same behaviors when on both sides of fear and love. You have to eat regardless of how you think or feel so notice if the kinds of food or amounts change. You may also enjoy things that seem to be unhealthy such as a cigar or glass of wine yet in moderate amounts they don't always have to have a negative impact. In those cases when you are partaking what is the feeling represented? Are you trying to escape something or cover up an emotion? Are you really just relaxing or celebrating? You may notice that when you are coming from Love you don't over consume as much as you would if you were doing it because you are upset. Too much of anything can represent an addiction which is always a fear based idea.

Take care to be honest with yourself and try not to be judgmental. This will just keep you in fear longer. Fear-based thoughts and behaviors are a signal. Try to listen and act accordingly. Sometimes we need the down time of being stuck. When you are ready to let it go, work toward things on the loving side of your Compass. If you need to you can go to your Backup Plan or the Tips for Tough Times Section to help you change your direction.

My Compass

LOVE
Growing Foward

Concious / Peaceful

Emotion

Healthy / Supportive

THOUGHTS

ACTIONS

Unconscious /Stressful

Survival Instinct
FEAR

Unhealthy / Sabotaging

Your Backup Plan

This is your list of supports that you can go to in times of stress or upset. In those moments it can be hard to think clearly and know what to do. We forget who we can call on, what we are good at and what can help us cope with what we are dealing with. It gets messy sometimes. When that happens you may need outside intervention. This is a plan when you find yourself feeling overwhelmed or alone.

<u>What is happening?</u>

On a physical level your body is responding from a place of survival. It shuts down to rational thought, physically sets you up to fight, flight or freeze in response to what you are doing. Emotionally you are slipping into that place of fear that can come out in many forms such as sadness, anger, shame, anxiety or other emotions. All of these are working against you. In this moment that you are stuck all is not lost. Remember who you really are is more than your feelings and your bodily response. On a spiritual, bigger picture level you can never be truly lost.

When dealing with Love and Fear remember you are dealing with states of being. Love being that which opens you to who you truly are, and fear, the state of being where you turn away from yourself to focus on a situation. Being in fear doesn't mean you can't get back to who you are, but it does make it harder to remember how to get there. This is bound to happen sometimes. This is the world we live in. You are still a human being dealing with very human things. Your Backup Plan will help you remember how to get back to yourself. It's not foolproof, it will take effort and it may need to be modified, but it's a start.

In this section fill in your favorite ideas to help yourself when you are having a tough time. This will be your reminder on days when it is hard to think clearly. Review your Profile and Use the Tips for Tough Times section to get ideas. As always, if you are in danger call emergency services immediately.

My Backup Plan

Who I call when I am upset:

_____
_____
_____
_____
_____
_____
_____

What I can do to relax:

_____
_____
_____
_____
_____
_____
_____

What I can do to lift my mood:

_____
_____
_____
_____
_____
_____

My Backup Plan

What I can do to improve my thinking:

_____
_____
_____
_____
_____
_____
_____

What helps me remember why I am making this change:

_____
_____
_____
_____
_____
_____
_____

Other Things I can Do:

1. Review your Profile and remember what you have survived in the past.

2. See the Tips for Tough Times section for further ideas.

3. Remember, you are not as stuck as you feel right now. You always have a choice. Choose to do something. If that doesn't work choose again and if need be ask for help.

_____
_____

Tips for Tough Times

The following tips are a way to give focus and work with your body's natural responses. They are meant to help you organize your thoughts and keep you moving toward your goal, a way to coach yourself out of a bad day or an unproductive thought pattern. If you are experiencing extreme stress or prolonged painful emotional responses these suggestions will not replace medical care or mental health counseling.

A must read prior to working with tips:

On the way to your goal you will experience some days that are less than perfect. Change is hard and can bring out unplanned stress and emotion. This does not mean it's time to give up, but rather that it's time to listen. Stress and emotional responses are your body's way of communicating that something is not right. Paying attention to that will help you move through those feelings and reactions sooner.

It is very important to honor what your body is telling you. For prolonged stress please seek medical help. It's important to take the time to get your body healthy so that you will have the strength you need to fully step into your goal.

If you are feeling painful emotions that will not lift in a reasonable amount of time, they may need to be worked through with a professional counselor.

If you have to pause here all is not lost. What you are experiencing is a natural part of your process. Facing what you need to now will actually help you get to your goal faster. If you were to skip over this it will come up again and possibly in a more aggressive way. This book is your personalized plan that can go with you and be utilized however you need.

If at any time you are having thoughts of harming yourself or someone else please call your local emergency services immediately.

How Stress and Emotion can help you meet your goal:

Understanding the function of stress and emotion is the first step toward managing it. We need our bodily responses to give us direction and to help us survive. The mind and the body are so inseparable it is important to really grasp what they are saying to each other. Doing that will help to break unproductive communications that keep you from meeting your goal. This doesn't mean we ignore what we don't want to hear but rather that we listen for the message and then make a conscious decision about whether we want to attend to it or not. By listening to the message we can get the most accurate information to gauge the right next step. Failing to listen will only prolong discomfort or allow it to build momentum and come out stronger at a later time. Neither will help you move forward.

The mind-body connection is very complicated. For our purpose in support of your goal, I will be breaking it down into simple ideas you can work with in your everyday experience. The mission is to keep focus on your goal. The work you have done so far with your whole-self has been determining what is naturally next for you. If negative thoughts and responses are coming up it is your fear questioning your sense of direction. It's important to listen to what your fear has to say and then use these suggestions to help decide if that fear is worth acting on or something you want to let go. Remember feelings are your compass not your problem. Honoring them for what they are will help you release them once they have done their job.

I cannot say enough that this is an over generalization that will not be successful with extreme emotion or stress. These are basic ideas to shift negative thoughts but will not give space for in-depth reflection. If you want to know more about what is going on for yourself seek counseling; it is a great way to see how you came to the thought patterns you have. The more you know the more successfully you will be able to navigate your mind-body.

How to best work with these tips:

To work with the tips suggested here it helps to understand the definitions. Sometimes just getting clear with how stress and emotion work can be enough to offset reactions that get in the way of what you are trying to do. Since the brain is responsible for ultimately all thought and movement in the body, your emotions originate there as well. They are a series of chemicals that the brain fires when directed to do so. Those directions if not part of a chemical imbalance or disorder come from our thoughts which are based on our interpretation of what we experience. What we think will play out in our bodily responses every time.

Being human we have self-awareness and because of that we can learn to understand our bodily responses. When we are conscious we can adjust our thinking and therefore change our body's reaction. In the mind-body connection your vocabulary becomes very important. Words are your directives to the brain that start the bodily chain reaction. How you define these words is also crucial because your brain is following your command based on your interpretation of what you are saying.

Stress:

The physical reaction your body has to adjust to various situations. It is your physical warning that something needs to change. Without some degree of stress you would never be motivated to change and could not survive. You might feel stress in the form of hunger when you need to eat. You might feel it through your emotions, which tells you a situation is not right. You can also feel it when you are surprised by either positive or negative news. However you get there stress is your body trying to find balance during chaotic situations.

Emotion:

The chemical signal that is flushed though the body in response to the mind's interpretation of an outside circumstance. Emotional responses that are not clouded by a brain chemistry imbalance are really the physical expression of how you perceive what is going on around you. When we face outside stimulation the mind creates a visual image that we then assign language. We also assign meaning to the situation and out of that comes our emotional response. This happens very quickly and much of the time without our awareness. These responses are the body's way of coping and adjusting to what we are living through in order to find balance.

Even though we have many different interpretations of our emotions based on our experience, the body will physically express them in one of two directions with varying intensity. Feelings such as frustration, worry or anger rev the body up where feelings such as sadness, shame or self-doubt slow the body down. All the different emotions we feel fall into some degree of these very over simplified physical responses. Identifying which direction your body is moving in will help you decide what course of action is best for you.

Using this information to move forward:

Having solid definitions will help you streamline your thinking in the way that will be more efficient. First assess whether you need to calm down or re-energize your body. Then go to the corresponding section with questions that will be help to assess your body's needs and give a direction for how to proceed. It is important not to skip over the questions because your body likes routine. That is how you got to the pattern of thought you are in. Negative thoughts get established over time and then become a habit that we are not always aware. These questions will not only increase your awareness but also give your mind another frame of reference to respond. Just like a computer will put whatever you type on the screen, your thoughts will have an immediate response in the body. A negative thought will have a similar response in the body. A new productive thought will give new productive results.

You will find that certain suggestions will overlap between calming and reenergizing tips. This is because some healthy thoughts and actions can do both depending on the way you use them. You will find specific ideas to work with both in each section. There is also a General List of other ideas at the end. Remember you are in charge. There are no wrong attempts. Trying something will either work well or give you more insight on what you really need. You can then use that information to try again. Each step can't help but move you forward.

Calming Your Body

When you feel stressed remember your body is telling you something. By asking these questions you answer your body's call and allow it to calm down faster. If you skip questions you ignore your body's internal dialogue and may miss important information. You need your stress to determine danger. Forgetting to ask or ignoring that first impulse can set up a pattern in the brain that avoids the original signal and may put you in danger.

When stressed, first ask yourself:
Am I in immediate danger?

If Yes:
Take action. Do what is necessary for your situation.

If No:
You are dealing with a worry or a perceived threat and so have time to think ahead about what to do.

Use this time to ask yourself:
Is this something I can control?

If Yes:
Determine what you could do to change the situation and take action. Gathering information, being proactive or changing habits can keep stress from happening in the first place.

If No:
It's time to plan ahead for the worst case scenario. This will tell the brain you have heard the message and with a plan your brain knows it is all clear to calm down. Even if it's not a perfect plan that guarantees success your mind will know that you have done all you can and therefore doesn't have a survival need to keep thinking about it.

It is natural for the brain to worry about the unknown. This is one of our basic ways to survive so we don't have to always rely on trial and error. With this we don't need to step into traffic without looking to find out what happens because we can imagine getting hit if we did.

If thoughts persist beyond the survival need its ok to let them go. Proceed to Relaxation Tips.

Relaxation Tips

1. **Take deep breaths-** Deep focused breaths fill the abdomen as well as the lungs, sending a direct signal to the brain to relax. Deep belly breaths are difficult to do when you are in a stress response because your body restricts your breathing to your lungs to get ready to fight or flight. You are going to have to go against what your body is doing in order to send a different signal. Focus your attention on your belly and as you breathe in, work your muscles to expand it like a balloon. This is much different than your stressed breathing which is going through your chest already. If you are finding it difficult to fully breathe in force yourself to fully exhale first to make room. Quick breaths or hyperventilating fill your lungs too quickly and then leave no room for a deep breath. Eventually, you will find your rhythm and find that you can initiate your breathe to start from your belly and then roll up to your chest. This is a more relaxed breath. The kind you breathe when you are sleeping. Once you start breathing that way your brain will register that it is time to relax. If you can make the effort and stay with it you will see results.

2. **Meditation-** Is the act of focusing on one thing at one time. You have many options besides sitting in silence. You can do a movement meditation like walking or practice being mindful during everyday activities. You can focus on your breaths or concentrate on an object. You can even use your imagination to create a visualization. With your head clear of distractions and your focus in the present stress has less opportunity to stick around.

3. **Relax your muscles-** You can do a meditation that focuses on tightening your muscle groups one at a time. If you are in a pinch and need to act fast, simply tighten the muscles in your entire body more firmly than they already are being stressed and hold for a count of five seconds. Then slowly release and repeat as needed. You will find that when you release over tightened muscles you will trigger them to relax more than what they were when you started. If you have time you can also isolate different muscle groups and do them one at a time for the five seconds each. Start from top to bottom or vice versa.

4. **Exercise-** Moving your body can be a great way to relieve stress. Regular exercise can also help keep you from getting overstressed. Any kind of exercise you enjoy will do. When you are engaging your body in physical exercise it can't maintain the stress response. Good amounts of regular exercise also release endorphins that can help improve your mood and helps to reduce stress.

5. **Know your stressors-** The more you know about your stress triggers the better you can prevent or cope with them. Things like too much caffeine or alcohol can be a problem and so they could be avoided. Not getting enough sleep or too much junk food can also contribute, so better habits can help. Other things like time management habits such as over-scheduling or procrastination can be changed. Even certain topics of conversation or activities that are upsetting can sometimes be avoided. It's important to look at your environment and listen to your body. The information is there if you are open to it. Even those things that can't be avoided can sometimes be made less intensive by planning in supports during stressful times.

6. **Take a time out-** It's okay to step away from your stressor and allow yourself to calm down. It can take the body as little as 3-5 minutes with some practice. A quick bathroom break could do the trick. A walk outside or in a different room can provide a nice change and help you get your body back on track.

7. **Find a distraction-** Do something you enjoy for a while. Reading, writing, music, cooking, playing sports, etc. You may also engage your mind with a rote activity such as a puzzle, a chore, a counting activity or maybe organizing something. Anything that you do to take focus off your stressor can give your body a rest.

8. **Use your senses-** Another way to distract from your stress is to do something that uses one or more of your five senses. Looking at something pleasant can give your mind something else to process besides your stressor. You can also use touch to change your focus. A massage, a bath, a comforting object, a blanket or maybe petting an animal are good possibilities. Smell can be very powerful as well. Enjoying the smell of the outdoors, a candle, a warm beverage or maybe cologne can be very distracting from stress. Listening to music or any soothing sound can be another great way to let go of stress. Music, nature sounds, wind chimes or any rhythmic noise can be a good escape. Don't be afraid to experiment and find something that works for you.

9. **Tell someone about it-** What you find stressful can be very different from someone else. Talking to someone can help to see things from a different perspective. Whether it is a friend or a professional the goal is to reframe your view of the situation so that you can manage your situation and your body's symptoms. Maybe your expectations are too high or you need to see the opportunity in a situation instead of focusing on the negatives. You may also need to see what is within your

control and let go of focusing on what you can't. There are many ways to interpret a situation and the one you choose will directly affect how your body responds.

10. **Create a routine of relaxation-** A great way to reduce stress is to plan regular amounts of fun. Connect with others and make plans to do things. Find reasons to laugh. A joke, a sitcom or even laughing at yourself can be very helpful. It's very important to make time to relax and do things you enjoy every day. Even if you only have a few minutes you need to make that a priority.

Shifting Stressful Thoughts

1. **Focus on what's happening now**- Worry cannot exist in the present moment. If you are worrying you are using your mind to create an image of what might happen or visualizing a memory of what already did. Either way you are using your imagination. This is not something that is happening right now. If any of what you are thinking was really happening you would not have time to worry because you would be too busy reacting. You can find the present by noticing what's going around you. One way to do that is to use your five senses. Examine what you see, hear, taste, touch and smell. You can also ask yourself who am I with, where am I, why am I here, when did I get here and how did I arrive. Anything you can do to bring awareness to the present will turn off the focus on your imagination.

2. **Turn on your left brain**- In theory, your brain can symbolically be divided into two halves, the right and the left. Right brain function includes emotions, creativity, intuition and your imagination. The left brain function has more to do with language, logic, critical thinking and reasoning. If you are experiencing stress or worry, you are using your imagination which is housed in the right brain. Both sides of the brain cannot be fully engaged at the same time, so if you know you are using your right side you can shut that down by finding something to do from your left side. These are activities that use your sense of logic and reasoning. Puzzles, counting, reading and organizing something are good places to start.

3. **Remember the facts**- Since worry relies on your imagination, another way to step out of that is to remember the facts. What do you really know about what is stressing you? What facts do you have that point to your worry really happening? Are you assuming something about someone that may not be true? What do statistics say about the probability of what you are afraid of really happening? In thinking logically your fear may turn out to be less scary than you thought. You might find that what you are thinking might happen is not very probable. You might also notice that what you thought someone said or did was not accurate at all. Facts that cannot be argued can really help sort through what is important to consider worrying about and what can be let go.

4. **Best and neutral case scenario**- When you are worrying you are already thinking the worst case scenario. It may be helpful to give your mind a second opinion. Even if it is far-fetched it will give your brain another thought to think about and therefore create another less stressful response in the body. For example: Say you are worried about strangers on the bus. You could imagine riding the bus watching another

passenger put a briefcase on the floor next to them. A possible worst case scenario is that there is a bomb inside. Another idea is a best case scenario that there is a large sum of money inside designated for charity. Just imagining this, even though you don't think it's entirely probable, can shift your mind and in turn change how your body reacts. Finally, ask yourself what is the most neutral situation. The neutral and most probable scenario is that the briefcase is full of paperwork for a job. Giving your mind other ideas to think about will help keep it from getting stuck on the negative one.

5. **Find gratitude**- A very powerful distraction is exploring what is working in your life. Remember what you are stressing over is just a part of your vast existence. There are many other life areas to focus on. You could also step back and ask yourself if this will still be important in a month or a year? If you look across your whole life there has to be something you are grateful for. It could be something you learned, a person or pet or maybe even something simpler like your favorite food. If you can't find one in yourself think about someone else less fortunate and see if that helps uncover what you might be grateful for in your life. Even acknowledging something small can shift your body away from stress.

6. **Visualization**- If you can imagine what you are afraid of you can also use your imagination to create a visual in your mind of something that makes you happy or feels calming. Anything that you put into your thoughts has a direct and immediate response in the body even if you don't fully believe it. You'll notice this when you are watching a scary movie and feeling afraid even though you know you are really safe. On one level you know that it is not real but your mind still got input that something scary was happening and reacted anyway. The same can be true in reverse. Putting something pleasant in your mind can evoke a more positive feeling than the fear you have when you are worried. It may not last long so you have to keep at it. You have to be more persistent and more repetitive than your fearful thoughts.

7. **Talk to yourself**- You can be your own coach by repeating a positive statement to yourself. Positive thoughts can trigger positive responses in the brain which will offset the not so pleasant ones. The chemical reaction related to a stressful thought takes about 90 seconds to circulate the body. What keeps you feeling stressed are additional stressful thoughts. When we get stuck and keep thinking about what upsets us we flush another chemical response through the body. Each additional thought is another flush. We can stop that when we change our thoughts. Finding

an inspirational statement to repeat to yourself can help balance positive chemical flushes with the negative ones lessening your emotional response. This can be a favorite quote, a song or your own words. Try to use phrases that remind you of your sense of peace and balance. Stating something you are grateful for is also very powerful. Repetition is important here. You have to build momentum with what you are saying with so try to increase your enthusiasm about what you are saying so you can override your stress response.

Reenergizing Your Body

When you feel down your body is giving you a signal that something has changed or needs to be different. These questions can help you assess and work with the message your body's is trying to convey. Your emotions are there for a reason if you skip questions you ignore your body's internal dialogue and may misunderstand what you need.

When feeling down, first ask yourself:
Am I in immediate danger of hurting myself or others?

If Yes:

Take action. Seek help from your local Emergency Services.

If No ask yourself:
Is this something I can control?

If No:

Take an honest look at what this feeling is trying to say. Are you in a situation that needs to change? Do you need more focus on taking better care of yourself? Is something you are afraid of coming up and triggering this response? Are you needing time to grieve?

If it is difficult to identify your feeling or what it means this would be a good time to talk to a counselor. They can be very helpful with another objective perspective that may help you figure out the message.

If Yes:

Determine what you could do to change the situation and take action. Good self-care, asking for help and keeping a healthy focus can help keep you from getting stuck

Once you identify the message you can use that info to ask again:
What about this is in my control?
If it is something you can control having a plan can be helpful. Even if it is something that can't be fixed right away acknowledging where you are and what you need to do next can help lift your motivation.

If you are not in danger of harm and have a plan the signal behind your emotion has been heard. Now the feeling can be let go of. Proceed to motivation tips.

Motivation Tips

1. **Know what you are up against-** As long as you are feeling down it will be hard to feel right about doing what you need to do to feel better until you start doing it. Feelings are a chemical response in the body. Whatever emotion you identify with, feeling down changes your body chemistry, just like worry induces a stress response. The function of this is to allow time for your body to catch up to an upsetting situation. It's healthy to allow your feeling and take time to let your body rest. It can become a problem if you feel down too long and it gets in the way of moving forward.

   Working with down feelings means stepping up and combating the body's chemical urge to stay down, to combat the urge with a different logic. The more you know about your emotion the more ammunition you have to fight it. The best defense against feeling down is doing the opposite of what you feel.

2. **Make a schedule-** If you are coping with a situation it can be helpful to allow time to let yourself be upset. Ignoring it can build it up and make you feel worse. If you find that too much time has gone by being upset it's important to encourage yourself to do other things as well. Making a schedule can help. Give yourself a certain amount of time to have your emotion and then plan another activity. Make plans with friends and keep appointments even if you don't feel like socializing. In order to get out of the negative cycle you have to do something different from what your body is telling you. You can even schedule your personal activities for the day. Feeling down can get in the way of motivating you to do even the basics. Giving yourself a simple To Do list of daily tasks can help you increase motivation. It can also be a nice feeling to cross things off.

3. **Get your body moving-** Despite having low energy you must keep moving. Staying still will just keep you feeling tired. Exercise can really help lift your mood. Research shows that moderate intensity aerobic exercise done at least 30 minutes per day 5 or more days per week can increase feel good chemicals in the brain. This includes serotonin which is linked to mood. Any kind of exercise can work so find one that you enjoy or can at least tolerate and then get started. Even small amounts to start will help.

4. **Know your triggers-** The more you know about what upsets you the better you can prevent or cope with it. Things that are upsetting can sometimes be avoided

with proper planning. Even things that can't be avoided can sometimes be made less intensive by planning in supports during upsetting times.

5. **Give yourself a reality check-** Feeling down can sometimes be a free license for your mind to wander into extreme thinking. When you are upset it can shape how you see a situation giving focus to the worse possible scenario. It's very important to remember the reality within your thoughts. If you are thinking "I am always doing something wrong," or "Something good never happens," you are thinking in the extremes which is hardly ever really the case. Work on scaling down your thoughts to what is really in front of you. There are more grey areas around situations than there are black and white. Explore the grey. You may also notice you are over-generalizing what's happening. You might expect what you are feeling to last forever or that your situation cannot change. Your body is designed to find balance and will continue to work on that despite what's going on. Follow that lead and work on the idea that deep down there are other options. Even if you don't find them right away making the effort can build momentum with your motivation may help with your mood.

6. **Visualization-** If you can imagine what you are looking for you are one step closer to having it. It may feel like a fantasy right now but if you can put the pieces together in your mind you will not only distract yourself from what you are upset about you will also open yourself up to be more creative about solutions. Even better write it down. If you don't know what you want first list what you don't want. When you are done go back over the list and write the opposite of what you don't want, which will then be what you do want. Imagining what it will be like can shift your motivation and offer hope. Anything that you put into your thoughts has a direct and immediate response in the body even if you don't fully believe it. You'll notice this when you are watching a sad movie and feeling the same sadness as the main character even though it's not really happening to you. On one level you know that it is not real but your mind still received input that something sad was happening and reacted anyway. The same can be true in reverse. Putting something hopeful in your mind can evoke a more positive feeling than the negative one you have now. It may not last long so you have to keep at it. You have to be more persistent and more repetitive than your negative thoughts.

7. **Talk to yourself-** You can be your own coach by repeating a positive statement to yourself. Positive thoughts can trigger positive responses in the brain which will offset the not so pleasant ones. The chemical reaction in the body related to a negative thought takes about 90 seconds to circulate the body. What keeps you feeling down is additional negative thoughts. When we get stuck and keep thinking

about what upsets us we flush another chemical response through the body. Each additional thought is another flush. We can stop that when we change our thoughts. Finding an inspirational statement to repeat to your self can help balance positive chemical flushes with the negative ones lessening your emotional response. This can be a favorite quote, a song or your own words. Try to use phrases that remind you of your power and wisdom. Stating something you are grateful for is also very powerful. Repetition is important here. You have to build momentum with what you are saying with so try to increase your enthusiasm about what you are saying so you can override your emotion.

Shifting Unproductive Thoughts

1. **Identify your thoughts-** See if you can listen to the voice in your head, that monologue that is constantly going on informing you of what's going on and how you feel. Sometimes it has positive things to say but if you are feeling down odds are that it is negative. See if you can pick out any themes such as "I am so stupid," "I look horrible," or "I am always alone." These are the thoughts that are shaping the way you see yourself and your world. They are also feeding your emotional response. It's good to take inventory and then prepare an opposing argument. Whatever negative thought you are having and think the opposite in response. Each though has a direct response in the body. Giving your brain a positive thought will give your body a chance to receive some positive chemicals instead of just the negative ones it is already getting. It is the beginning of balancing the chemical scale.

2. **Remember the facts-** Feeling down thrives on negative thinking. Allowing your mind to get lost in such thinking can make matters worse. Try not to make negative conclusions without evidence to support them. Thoughts like "They must not like me," "I'll be stuck in this place," and "He must be out to get me," are not necessarily completely true. Also just because you are having a feeling doesn't mean it will really have impact on your life. It may be that you are making assumptions about someone or something. Expand your search to include what's real, what is most probable and what might even be positive. When you are down your mind will hyper-focus on the negative facts and filter out the positive or neutral ones. It will also go one step further and come up with its own reasoning to determine that your positive solutions won't work. Investigate further. There is always more than you can see.

3. **Focus on what's happening now-** If you are thinking negative thoughts you are using your mind to create an image of a bad situation or visualizing a memory of one. Either way you are using your imagination. While the situation might be real keeping all your focus in your imagination and replaying it can keep you stuck. Focusing on the tangible present can be a good and realistic distraction. You can find the present by noticing what's going around you. One way to do that is to use your five senses. Examine what you see, hear, taste, touch and smell. You can also ask yourself who am I with, where am I, why am I here, when did I get here and how did I arrive. Anything you can do to bring awareness to the present will turn off the focus on your imagination.

4. **Meditation-** Is the act of focusing on one thing at one time. You have many options besides sitting in silence. You can also do a movement meditation like walking or practice being mindful during everyday activities. You can focus on your breaths or use an object to concentrate on. You can even use a visualization using your imagination. When you feel down you can use this time to reflect and ask for creative solutions. You can also invite spiritual support or contemplation. Some people find that after quiet moments they can see things in a different way. Keeping a journal of your thoughts can help track ideas.

5. **Find a distraction-** Since feeling down will work to keep you stuck the best thing you can do is anything that will keep you moving forward. Sabotaging behaviors such as sleeping all day, binging, using alcohol or drugs or avoiding people will keep your down feelings going. It's a vicious cycle. You feel bad so you care less about yourself and then do things that, although feel good for a while, end up leaving you disappointed and feeling worse. That then becomes the perfect excuse to be down again and the cycle goes on and on. Again you are not going to wake up and feel like doing anything different but if you want change you are going to have to. Starting is the hardest part. Once you get moving your momentum will help you keep going. Take the first step now. Go out for a walk, meet a friend, seek out a support group, read an uplifting book, watch a comedy, do something creative, cook a healthy meal. Do something, anything but what you have been doing. See General Mood Lifting Ideas for suggestions.

6. **Turn on your left brain-** In theory your brain can symbolically be divided into two halves the right and the left. If you are experiencing unproductive thoughts you are using your imagination to visualize something you don't want or feel bad about. These thoughts are housed in the right brain. Right brain function includes emotions, creativity, intuition and your imagination. The left brain function has more to do with language, logic, critical thinking and reasoning. Both sides of the brain cannot be fully engaged at the same time so if you know you are using your right side you can shut that down by finding something to do from you left side. These are activities that use your sense of logic and reasoning. Puzzles, counting, reading and organizing something are good places to start. Your goal is to step out of your imagination and focus on something tangible that has a sense of order.

7. **Find gratitude-** A very powerful distraction is exploring what is working in your life. Remember what you are upset over is just a part of your vast existence. There are many other life areas to focus on. You could also step back and ask yourself if this will still be important in a month or a year? If you look across your whole life there has to be something you are grateful for. It could be something you learned,

a person or pet or maybe even simpler like your favorite food. If you can't find one in yourself think about someone else less fortunate and see if that helps uncover what you might be grateful for in your life. Even acknowledging something small can shift your body away from painful emotion.

8. **Express your feelings**- Finding creative ways to express your feelings can help keep them from coming out in the wrong way. The arts, writing, and music are all helpful outlets. Anything that you can do to bring joy in your life can create more balance and less painful emotion. Humor can also play an important role. Laughter and feeling down cannot coexist.

9. **Communicate your feelings**- Talking about your feelings can help keep unproductive thoughts from building up over time. Learning where your feelings stems from is vital to keep it from becoming a pattern. Expressing yourfeelings will also help others understand you and what you need. They can't workwith you otherwise. Not only do you need to express your feelings but you alsoneed to turn your complaints into requests. If you don't request a change it harderfor something new happen. Using language like "You always do this," or "You never do that," will only serve to create tension with the person you are trying to talk to. When trying to communicate it's best to start with how you are feeling.

Example:

When you _____ I feel_____ because_____
Please do or say_____instead.

Once you make a request it's important that you stand behind it with a plan about what you will do if your request is not followed up on.

Example:

If you_____then I will_____

This is not an excuse to be aggressive with someone but rather a reminder that you are responsible for your own happiness. We can't change other people we can only change ourselves. If you are not getting what you need it's up to you to make the appropriate changes to take care of yourself.

General Mood Lifting Ideas

These are general suggestions of things to do to feel better. Sometimes when we feel down or stressed it can be hard to come up with new ideas. You are not alone. This list is from a variety people who have been able to shift their mood by doing these things. Hopefully you will find relief from one of them as well. If not please ask for help. Call your doctor, a therapist or if you are having thoughts of harming yourself your local Emergency Services.

Talk to yourself

Remember you have the power to understand and get through this

Listen to music or read a book

Watch a sitcom or comedy show

Eat fun, comforting foods in moderation

Take a bath or shower by candle light

Dance, Sing or try Yoga

Learn to say "No"

Tolerate uncomfortable feelings for just a little while longer than before

Talk to a friend

Enjoy a hobby

Read or watch something inspiring

Exercise

Find something or someone to be thankful for

Take time for yourself

Leave a bad situation

Sit in the sunlight

Review your goals and resolutions

Help someone else in need

Expect growth to feel uncomfortable

Allow yourself to cry

Cook something yummy

Spend time with an animal

Join a club or community group

Investigate other options

Go for a drive

Be kind to your body do something healthy

Take a nap

Eat chocolate

Break down larger tasks into smaller ones

Visit nature

Change a habit

Focus on the present moment

Vent your anger in a letter then tear it up

Reward yourself

Take responsibility for what's yours and give the rest away

Ask for help

Have a hot beverage

Build or craft something

Remind yourself that there are other options you haven't seen yet

Seek understanding

For every negative thought fight back with a positive one

Play a game

Learn about something new

Do something childish and fun

Get a pet

Call someone you haven't talked to in a while

Smile Anyway

Meditate

Go to a place of worship

Organize something

Read or write poem

Find something to do with each of your five senses

Send a card to someone

Draw or doodle something

Remember you are more than your thoughts, feelings or behaviors

Breathe

Set a schedule for yourself

Talk to your higher power

Pretend the situation is better and write yourself a letter about what it is like

Spend some time with a child

Set a new intention

Join a support group

Volunteer

Just Try Something- Anything

One more thought:

If you are still having trouble changing your mood, try looking outside yourself. Can you find anything that is beautiful or loving in some small way? Set out on a mission to find something that you can appreciate. A tree, an old building, a child's smile, a nice car, a piece of art, a beautifully plated meal, a city skyline, a happy couple, whatever looks good to you. Even if it is something you are wishing for see the positive in it. If you can see it and make sense of it then that beauty, that positive feeling, has to exist within you. Your brain wouldn't be able to put those thoughts together if it didn't. Remember Key Concept # 11:

Embracing your true self
is like looking into
the most beautiful sunset
and realizing it's your own reflection

If you can do nothing else just remember that who you really are is still intact no matter what you are thinking and feeling or what is going on around you.

Seeing something positive is the first step to feeling it.

For more information

Lauri currently assists individuals and groups with coaching and counseling sessions at her Westerly, Rhode Island office. She is also available online for both individual coaching sessions and group classes.

If you are a professional interested in learning more about how to use this process with your clientele, please contact Lauri for more information on her newest workbook:

Growing The Whole Way
A Teaching Guide for Coaches and Counselors

This workbook teaches about what holism is and how to foster that perspective in your work. It also instructs how to best utilize the Growing The Whole Way structure to ground client goals, organize the process needed for change, and assess what clients need after sessions are complete.

You will learn:

- How to align the program to your specialty and meet client specific needs.
- What is behind the key concepts that help your clients think bigger so that you can effectively teach them.
- Strategies on how to use holism to increase client motivation and follow through.
- Helpful tips to work with your own self-care and efficiency in your work.

For contact information or class schedule visit GrowingTheWholeWay.com

Additional books are also available at Amazon.com

Made in United States
North Haven, CT
08 September 2022

23826995R00085